This book belongs to

.Lorna. H...

Pidgins and

G000134238

½)

To: Dearest Lorna,
One of my favourite
students! Read well!
Love,
Ishtla

Pidgins and Creoles

An introduction

ISHTLA SINGH

Lecturer in English Language and Linguistics,
University of Surrey Roehampton

A member of the Hodder Headline Group
LONDON
Co-published in the United States of America by
Oxford University Press Inc., New York

First published in Great Britain in 2000 by
Arnold, a member of the Hodder Headline Group,
338 Euston Road, London NW1 3BH

http://www.arnoldpublishers.com

Co-published in the United States of America by
Oxford University Press Inc.,
198 Madison Avenue, New York 10016

The advice and information in this book are believed to be true and accurate at
the date of going to press, but neither the author nor the publisher can accept
any legal responsibility or liability for any errors or omissions.

British Library Cataloguing in Publication Data
A catalogue record for this book is available from the British Library

Library of Congress Cataloging-in-Publication Data
A catalog record for this book is available from the Library of Congress

ISBN 0 340 70094 7 (hb)
ISBN 0 340 70095 5 (pb)

1 2 3 4 5 6 7 8 9 10

Production Editor: Anke Ueberberg
Production Controller: Iain McWilliams
Cover Design: Terry Griffiths

Typeset in 11/13pt Sabon by Phoenix Photosetting, Chatham, Kent
Printed and bound in Great Britain by MPG Books Ltd, Bodmin, Cornwall

What do you think about this book? Or any other Arnold title?
Please send your comments to feedback.arnold@hodder.co.uk

He looked into the water and saw that it was made up of a thousand thousand thousand and one different currents ... a liquid tapestry of breathtaking complexity; and Iff explained that these were the Streams of Story, that each coloured strand represented and contained a single tale. ... And because the stories were held here in liquid form, they retained the ability to change, to become new versions of themselves, to join up with other stories and so become yet other stories; so that the Ocean of Streams of Story was ... not dead but alive.

(Salman Rushdie *Haroun and the Sea of Stories*)

Contents

Acknowledgements

The author and publishers would like to thank the following for permission to use copyright material in this book:

The Barbados Tourism Authority for the advertisement 'Barbados Crop Over Festival is here again', Trinidad Guardian (24/7/99); Mahase Calpu and the Trinidad Express for the cartoons 'Sweetbread' (18/7/99) and 'Patrick, if dis eh work' (3/6/99); Cambridge University Press and John Holm for maps of pidgins and creoles worldwide in *Introduction to Pidgins and Creoles*. Textbooks in Linguistics. Cambridge: Cambridge University Press; Cambridge University Press for David DeCamp 'Towards a Generative Analysis of a Post Creole Speech Continuum' in Dell Hymes (ed.) (1971) *Pidginization and Creolization of Languages*, pp. 349–370; Penguin for Salman Rushdie (1990) *Haroun and the Sea of Stories* (Granta Books, copyright Salman Rushdie 1990), p. 72; Trinidad Publishing Company Ltd for the Trinidad Guardian, 'From Our Files: Evidence in Patois' (reprinted 7/7/97) and 'From Our Files: Courses for Teachers' (reprinted 14/6/97).

There are many people who, in lots of different ways, helped make this book happen and who therefore deserve big 'thank-yous': April McMahon, who first suggested that I should write it (and who believed I could do it!); my colleagues at the University of Surrey Roehampton for their continued encouragement; Linda Thomas for her unshakeable support; Jen Coates and Jason Jones for reading the manuscript; my students Alison Heard, Lesley Hodgson and Helen Jamieson for feedback on chapters; Kate, Sarah and Wendy for their constant affirmation of what I was doing; my parents for their invaluable help in tracking down copyright holders in Trinidad; and last but by no means least, Andrew Pitman for myriad cups of tea, help with computers, unwavering belief in me and incredible patience.

Preface

This book grew out of a 12-week course, *Pidgins and Creoles*, which I teach to second- and third-year English Language and Linguistics undergraduates at the University of Surrey Roehampton. Many of my students sign up for the course because a brief encounter with the subject in one or two of their other modules has left them with a desire to find out more about the whys and wherefores of pidgins and creoles. I'm pleased to say that quite a few of them go on to do extended essays or dissertations on them as well, having caught the bug, so to speak!

This is not always an easy task – many of my students have found a great deal of the literature to which they have access either too introductory or too difficult (in that it sometimes assumes a more than elementary knowledge of the field). One of the main aims of this book is to attempt to bridge that gap: I have tried to move beyond introductory material, present salient theories and arguments in an accessible manner but yet not assume too much linguistic knowledge on the part of the reader. The way in which I have chosen to do this is to structure what I want to share with you into a narrative framework: in Chapter 1, we define our subject matter and try to give it a context in the wider field of linguistic enquiry; in Chapter 2, we look at different ideas of how pidgin and creole systems may have been born; Chapter 3 examines a model which was devised to account for a type of variation that occurs in communities with established creoles, and Chapter 4 details some of the socio-political issues that will impact on their future. You will notice that the names of Chapters 2–4 each begin with a different phrase. These are taken from story-telling conventions in my native Trinidadian creole. *Once long ago, not too long ago* (Chapter 2) is the opening line of *The Story of Pan*, an oral poem by Paul Keens Douglas, who often composes wholly in Trinidad's creole. *An' den de news spread across de lan'* (Chapter 3) introduces the middle section of another of his poems *Fedon's Flute*; and *Crick crack, monkey break 'e back for a piece of pommerac* (Chapter 4) traditionally signifies, in Trinidad, the end of a tale in oral story-telling.

In each of these chapters, I have tried (where relevant) to draw parallels between pidgins and creoles and other languages, in order to highlight either differences or similarities, because one of the things I hope to show you is that though these are distinctive systems, they are not unusual or atypical. For quite a long time, pidgin and creole studies were considered peripheral to linguistic enquiry; but they have increasingly become an area where some very innovative and interesting work, which often has repercussions for other linguistic disciplines, is taking place.

This is not to say that creolistics, as the study of pidgins and creoles is sometimes called, has produced any conclusive answers on any of the burning (or smouldering!) questions in linguistics (indeed, it will become clearer as you read through the chapters that very little is set in stone in pidgin and creole studies itself) but it has made linguists reconsider, or think more carefully about, certain issues. In fact, one of the comments the majority of my students make on completion of the course, is that it brings lots of different 'streams' together: they make connections with questions and data they have encountered in other courses on, for example, historical linguistics, sociolinguistics and language acquisition; and 'think about things that they've never had to before'. Thus, the study of pidgins and creoles brings linguistics alive in some way: as languages which cannot be satisfactorily examined without reference to the situations in which they were born and the speakers that keep them alive, they essentially remind us that the story of language evolution, contact, change and development (in other words, all the things that linguistics is concerned with) is really the story of ourselves.

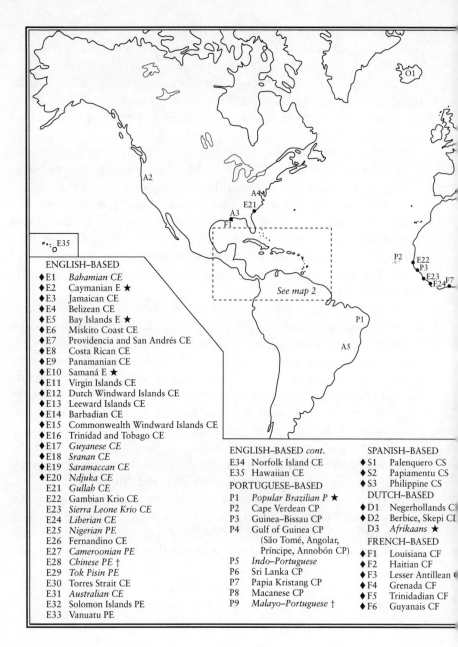

E35

ENGLISH–BASED
- ♦E1   *Bahamian CE*
- ♦E2   Caymanian E ★
- ♦E3   Jamaican CE
- ♦E4   Belizean CE
- ♦E5   Bay Islands E ★
- ♦E6   Miskito Coast CE
- ♦E7   Providencia and San Andrés CE
- ♦E8   Costa Rican CE
- ♦E9   Panamanian CE
- ♦E10 Samaná E ★
- ♦E11 Virgin Islands CE
- ♦E12 Dutch Windward Islands CE
- ♦E13 Leeward Islands CE
- ♦E14 Barbadian CE
- ♦E15 Commonwealth Windward Islands CE
- ♦E16 Trinidad and Tobago CE
- ♦E17 *Guyanese CE*
- ♦E18 *Sranan CE*
- ♦E19 *Saramaccan CE*
- ♦E20 *Ndjuka CE*
-   E21 *Gullah CE*
-   E22 Gambian Krio CE
-   E23 *Sierra Leone Krio CE*
-   E24 *Liberian CE*
-   E25 *Nigerian PE*
-   E26 Fernandino CE
-   E27 *Cameroonian PE*
-   E28 *Chinese PE* †
-   E29 *Tok Pisin PE*
-   E30 Torres Strait CE
-   E31 *Australian CE*
-   E32 Solomon Islands PE
-   E33 Vanuatu PE

ENGLISH–BASED *cont.*
- E34 Norfolk Island CE
- E35 Hawaiian CE

PORTUGUESE–BASED
- P1 *Popular Brazilian P* ★
- P2 Cape Verdean CP
- P3 Guinea–Bissau CP
- P4 Gulf of Guinea CP
      (São Tomé, Angolar,
      Príncipe, Annobón CP)
- P5 *Indo–Portuguese*
- P6 Sri Lanka CP
- P7 Papia Kristang CP
- P8 Macanese CP
- P9 *Malayo–Portuguese* †

SPANISH–BASED
- ♦S1 Palenquero CS
- ♦S2 Papiamentu CS
- ♦S3 Philippine CS

DUTCH–BASED
- ♦D1 Negerhollands C
- ♦D2 Berbice, Skepi CI
-   D3 *Afrikaans* ★

FRENCH–BASED
- ♦F1 Louisiana CF
- ♦F2 Haitian CF
- ♦F3 Lesser Antillean (
- ♦F4 Grenada CF
- ♦F5 Trinidadian CF
- ♦F6 Guyanais CF

See map 2

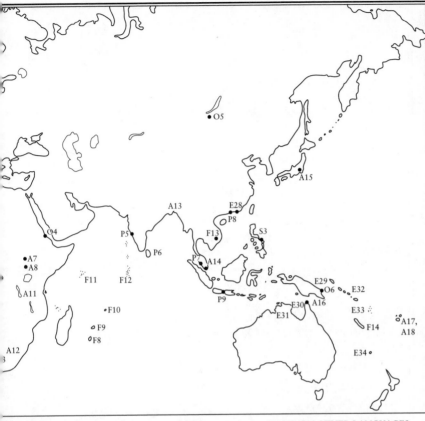

The map contains the following labels: O5, A15, A13, E28, P8, O4, P5, F13, S3, P6, A7, A8, F11, F12, P7, A14, E29, O6, E32, A11, F10, P9, E30, A16, E33, A17, A18, F14, A12, F9, F8, E31, E34

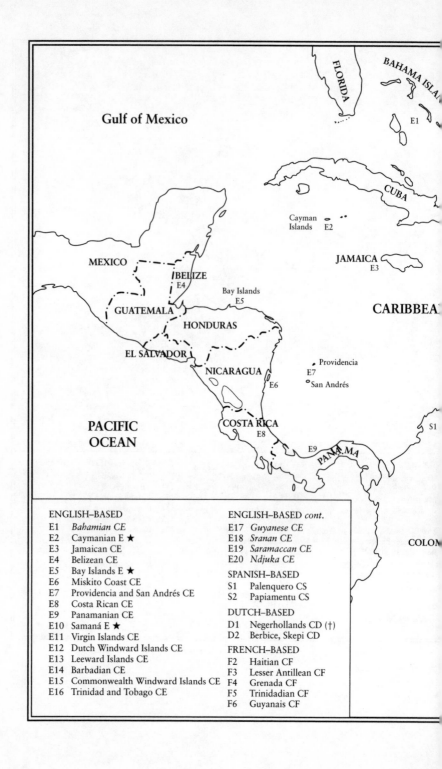

FLORIDA

BAHAMA ISLANDS

Gulf of Mexico

CUBA

Cayman
Islands   E2

JAMAICA
E3

E1

MEXICO

BELIZE
E4

Bay Islands
E5

CARIBBEAN

GUATEMALA

HONDURAS

EL SALVADOR

NICARAGUA

Providencia

E7

San Andrés

E6

PACIFIC
OCEAN

COSTA RICA
E8

S1

E9   PANAMA

COLOM

ENGLISH–BASED

E1	*Bahamian* CE
E2	Caymanian E ★
E3	Jamaican CE
E4	Belizean CE
E5	Bay Islands E ★
E6	Miskito Coast CE
E7	Providencia and San Andrés CE
E8	Costa Rican CE
E9	Panamanian CE
E10	Samaná E ★
E11	Virgin Islands CE
E12	Dutch Windward Islands CE
E13	Leeward Islands CE
E14	Barbadian CE
E15	Commonwealth Windward Islands CE
E16	Trinidad and Tobago CE

ENGLISH–BASED *cont.*

E17	*Guyanese* CE
E18	*Sranan* CE
E19	*Saramaccan* CE
E20	*Ndjuka* CE

SPANISH–BASED

S1	Palenquero CS
S2	Papiamentu CS

DUTCH–BASED

D1	Negerhollands CD (†)
D2	Berbice, Skepi CD

FRENCH–BASED

F2	Haitian CF
F3	Lesser Antillean CF
F4	Grenada CF
F5	Trinidadian CF
F6	Guyanais CF

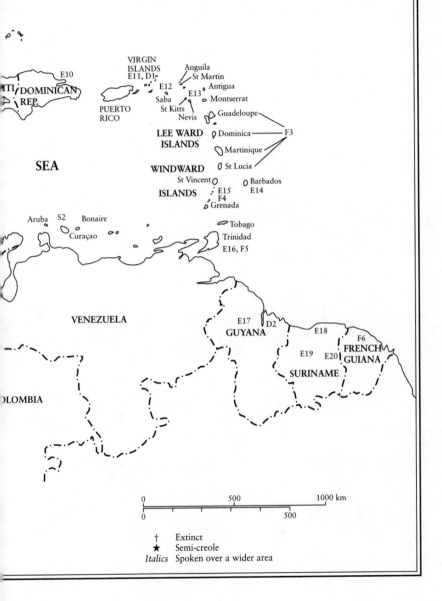

ATLANTIC
OCEAN

VIRGIN
ISLANDS
E11, D1
E12
Saba
St Kitts
Nevis

Anguila
St Martin
Antigua
E13
Montserrat
Guadeloupe

E10

TI DOMINICAN
REP.

PUERTO
RICO

LEE WARD
ISLANDS

Dominica ———— F3

Martinique

SEA

WINDWARD

St Lucia

St Vincent
ISLANDS

Barbados
E14

E15
F4
Grenada

Aruba   S2   Bonaire
Curaçao

Tobago
Trinidad
E16, F5

VENEZUELA

E17   D2
GUYANA

E18

E19   E20

F6
FRENCH
GUIANA

SURINAME

OLOMBIA

0   500   1000 km

0   500

†   Extinct
★   Semi-creole
Italics   Spoken over a wider area

1

Definitions

Once when we went to Europe, a rich old lady asked,
'Have you no language of your own?'

(Edward Brathwaite, *The Arrivants*)

1.1 Introduction

The enquiry made by Brathwaite's *rich old European lady* (a metaphor for an old, now possibly barren, colonial power) is directed to a young man from an ex-British, Caribbean territory (the developing, virile, New World culture) who speaks both his native creole and English. We can therefore assume that her question is double-pronged: she may be implying that his creole is not a language but instead a 'broken' appropriation of English; or that as a citizen of the New World (as opposed to the Old), he should not be using a language (English) that belongs to another culture. Brathwaite's narrator does not have an answer for his interrogator who essentially wonders, like many who know little about these languages and the societies they serve, 'what exactly is this creole and how "real", how useful is it?' As a native creole speaker, I think that the answer is an involved one, lying in the story of creoles and of creole studies. To understand what creole languages are and what makes them distinctive, we need to explore their history and look at the circumstances and the peoples that bring them into being. To understand their 'reality' as languages, we need to look not only at their linguistic viability but also at the kinds of issues and concerns their native speakers have. All of this constitutes a narrative that encompasses social histories, linguistic data, theories and postulations, and socio-political issues. Before 'settling in for the tale', however, we need to put their story into context. Section 1.2 therefore sets out a basic definition of a creole, and Section 1.3 looks at the role creoles have come to play in other areas of linguistic enquiry.

1.2 What is a creole?

Since creoles are often discussed in conjunction with *pidgins*, which are generally thought to be an early stage of creole development, we shall begin our definition there.

For many people, the term *pidgin* describes what is commonly perceived as 'broken' speech. For example, the attempts of non-fluent, non-native speakers of English to use that language to its native speakers for some specific purpose (such as asking for directions) is often described variously as *broken English, pidgin English* or *pidgin*. A general perception of *pidgin*, then, is that it is something that arises spontaneously in situations where communication between groups that speak mutually unintelligible languages is needed; and because it is unplanned it is also, by its very nature, random. In other words, it is often assumed that pidgins have no structural or grammatical rules to speak of.

To some extent, these perceptions are not totally untrue: linguists agree that pidgins are one outcome of language contact between speakers of different native languages who need to communicate. They are therefore sometimes termed *auxiliary languages*, since they 'help along' communication in such difficult circumstances. However, a lack of linguistic structure is not characteristic of a pidgin, although the latter may emerge out of a system that is 'unstable both linguistically and socially': a *jargon* (Mühlhäusler 1986: 147). Jargons, created and used in an ad hoc manner, show a high degree of lexical and grammatical variation from speaker to speaker. They also have a limited range of functions since they are often used for certain purposes only. A commonly cited example of a jargon (though not an uncontested one: see Romaine 1988: 124) is Russenorsk, once spoken by eighteenth- to early twentieth-century Russian sailors and Norwegian fishermen meeting for trade (on the Arctic coast of northern Norway) in the brief Arctic summer. The two groups therefore met annually for a very short space of time for a very specific purpose. However, in the periods of no contact, each group came to include new members and lose others. Thus, Russenorsk was essentially 're-created' each year (Sebba 1997: 63) for the same purpose. Such reconstitution of the system meant that aspects of its vocabulary, phonology and grammar were changeable, with variation largely being determined by the speaker's native tongue. For example, a Russian Russenorsk speaker might use *I* 'and', while a Norwegian might use *og*. Russian lacks the phoneme /h/, and so Russenorsk words with a Norwegian etymology, such as *hav* 'sea', would be pronounced by a Russian Russenorsk speaker as *gav.* The latter would also reduce Norwegian consonant clusters in accordance with Russian **phonotactic** rules: *mnogo li* 'many' would become *nogoli* (Holm 1989: 623–4).

As is evident in the case of Russenorsk speakers, the people who use a jargon need to speak to each other but do not constitute a stable speech community who together develop and share consistent linguistic norms. What they create instead in their jargon is a form of communication which mixes two systems: a *secondary hybrid* (Whinnom 1971). In biology, a *primary hybrid* is one which has had an uneventful evolution from one ancestral species; while *secondary hybrids* are the result of species interbreeding. Linguistics treats many of the world's languages as primary hybrids. English, for example, is classified as having evolved from West Germanic, which in itself is descended from Proto-Germanic, a daughter of Proto-Indo-European (see the discussion of the family tree model in Section 1.3). A form such as Russenorsk, which 'interbreeds' Russian and Norwegian, is therefore linguistically akin to the biological secondary hybrid. According to Whinnom (1971), a major reason why linguistic secondary hybrids, like some of their biological counterparts, are inherently unstable systems is because one set of speakers sees the language of the other group as a target (another name for Russenorsk, for example, is *moja pa tuoja* 'me according to you' or 'I talk in your way' (Thomason and Kaufman 1988: 167)), but may be unable to have unlimited access to it. Thus *Gastarbeiterdeutsch* 'guest-worker German', which is spoken in Germany by migrant workers from Mediterranean countries, can also be classed as a secondary hybrid. Many of these foreign workers inevitably view German as a target language, given their status as a minority group living and working in that country, but have no means of formally acquiring it. Consequently, their resultant *Gastarbeiterdeutsch* is viewed by some scholars as a jargon, or a 'collection of personal "versions" of German showing different degrees of success at second language learning' by individual migrant workers (Sebba 1997: 80).

It is possible that the social context that gave rise to many of the world's pidgins and creoles, that of slavery and colonization, also evolved secondary hybrids in early stages of contact. Initial contact between those with socio-political power (in this case, the Europeans: the **superstratal** group) and those with little or none (such as the African slaves: the **substratal** group) may have led to a

situation where the European language was set up as a 'model' for
the less powerful. Given the balance of power and the purposes of the
slave trade, European traders and slavers would have been unlikely
to spend time learning African tongues or teaching their own. They
would therefore have used their native European language in communication with the Africans who, in turn, would have had to
accommodate to this, all in a context of social distance and
undoubted hostility. Thus members of the substratal group would
not have had easy access to the superstratal target and, indeed, some
may not have fundamentally wanted it. The initial result of such
contact, therefore, would very likely have been jargons based heavily
on the superstratal language, but which would vary from substratal
speaker to speaker, depending on their access to, and motivation to
acquire, the presented target.

In some contact situations however, both linguistic and biological,
evolution continues with the involvement of other 'species'. This
Whinnom (1971) terms the *tertiary hybridization* process. In a
linguistic setting, this metaphorically refers to the use of the secondary
hybrid (or jargon) as a primary means of communication by a group
who do not speak the original target language, but who have no other
language in common. When this occurs, the jargon has to increase in
stability in order to adequately serve the needs of an emerging speech
community. Its speakers therefore begin to 'fix' their norms of usage.

Stabilization of a jargon, or tertiary hybridization, is under way
when the following linguistic processes begin to take place:

- the reduction of variability found in preceding jargon stages;
- the establishment of relatively firm lexical and grammatical conventions;
- the development of grammatical structures independent of possible source languages (that is, the creation of structures not based
  on those in speakers' native languages).

(after Mühlhäusler 1986: 176)

We can illustrate this with reference to our example of
European–African contact in the context of slavery. It is likely that a
jargon was used in the initial contact between European master and
African slaves, for specific purposes. However, in certain cases, such
as on the sugar and cotton plantations of the New World, substratal
groups frequently comprised speakers of different, often mutually
unintelligible languages since each plantation owner, working on the

premise of 'no communication, no revolution', often tried not to buy slaves from the same or related tribes. Slaves were also forbidden, on pain of punishment, from using their native languages once on plantations. Substratal speakers, therefore, had no language in common but were forced to live and work together. Given that the jargon was the only form of communication they had in common, it is highly likely that they began using it amongst themselves and so turned it (perhaps within the course of a generation) into a fairly stable form: a pidgin. The prerequisites for Whinnom's process of tertiary hybridization are clearly present here: the secondary hybrid (jargon) is turned into a more developed form by a community who do not natively speak the target (superstratal) language, but who are also linguistically diverse.

This tertiary hybrid, the pidgin, is likely to quickly replace the jargon as an *auxiliary language* between masters and slaves. Like its physical counterpart, the pidgin is a narrow 'bridge' that in connecting 'sides' (such as substratal speaker ↔ substratal speaker; substratal speaker ↔ superstratal speaker) also highlights the distance and the gap between them. In other words, a pidgin will allow diverse speakers to communicate but the very fact that it needs to be used reflects and maintains the socio-cultural and linguistic differences that obtain among its speakers. This is perhaps most true of substratal ↔ superstratal speaker communication: whereas the pidgin eventually comes to serve a 'bonding function' among the members of the substratal community shaping it, who are, after all, sharing a common social experience, it is unlikely to decrease the gap between its respective socially powerful and powerless speakers.

Sebba (1997: 54) states that pidgins, as relatively stable forms, tend to have the following general features.

1 *Lack of surface grammatical complexity.* Grammatical categories, such as plurals and past tense, for example, will not be signalled in speech. In addition, speakers may use invariant word order, so that questions in an English pidgin, for example, are signalled by intonation rather than by subject–verb inversion (as in *You see she?* vs *Did you see her?*). They will also use more coordination of clauses, as opposed to subordination.

2 *Lack of morphological complexity.* This is linked to the last point. The stock of inflectional morphology (which in many languages allows for plural and tense marking, for example) will be small. Speakers are unlikely to make use of derivational morphological

processes (comparable, for example, with the English '-er' suffix that derives nouns from verbs: *write → writer*).

3 *Semantic transparency*. Pidgin speakers will make use of compounds where the meanings are signalled quite explicitly by the morphemes used. For example, the equivalent of *where* in an English pidgin might be *what place*; of *why*, *what for*; of *tears, eye-water*; of *nostril, nose-hole*.

4 *Vocabulary reduction*. The pidgin will have a small stock of lexical items (typically 'short' words), including very few function words; that is, items such as pronouns and pre-/post-positions.

Pidgins are therefore not as linguistically complex as other languages. Their 'minimalist' structure is one of the reasons why many people think of pidgins as 'broken' versions of 'full' languages, and has led to their categorization as *simple* forms of communication. This is actually quite misleading, since *simple* in linguistics does not denote naivety but instead *grammatical regularity*. In other words, we could say that a language like English has a *simple* (or *regular*) number marking system in that the majority of plural forms are inflected with '-s'. Mühlhäusler (1986: 4) therefore suggests that pidgins should alternatively be described as *impoverished* systems, given their reduced structure.

Despite linguistic impoverishment, however, speakers of stable pidgins will follow norms of usage, though there is likely to be interference from individual native languages. If speakers restrict its use (for example, primarily to, and relaying, the limited communication between masters and slaves), then it will remain impoverished, since the 'emphasis is on the referential or communicative rather than the expressive function of language' (Romaine 1988: 24). However, if the majority of its speakers (such as the substratal community) continue to 'push' the pidgin, using it in an ever-increasing range of functions, its linguistic resources will also expand simultaneously. This is known as the *extension* or *expansion* phase, and it puts the pidgin 'on course to become a language, with the full referential and expressive capabilities of any other language' (Sebba 1997: 106). Its speakers may start to use it in new ways such as, for example, story-telling. They will therefore develop its linguistic and stylistic resources, so that it can effectively convey past, present and future imagined events; create colourful imagery and vivid characters; make use of metaphorical language and fulfil genres such as tragedy and romance – all this and more from a system that may have started life as a trading jargon!

Overall, expansion affects every level of structure: in terms of vocabulary and phonology, speakers come to use lexical items that are structurally more complex and to incorporate multifunctional terms (comparable with, for example, English *réject*_{noun}/*rejéct*_{verb}); in morphology and syntax, the use of derivational and inflectional processes increases, as does that of subordination in utterances, which in itself leads to the development and use of complementizers such as *which* or *that*. One of the major consequences of this is that speakers now have a range of stylistic options to choose from and so, essentially, have a language which they can use for a number of functions in many aspects of their daily lives.

At this point, the expanded pidgin is a short step away from becoming a creole and, indeed, many of the former's linguistic features are also characteristic of creoles. However, one of the crucial differences between the two is that pidgins have no native speakers, while creoles do. Thus, the first generation of an extended pidgin-speaking community that adopts it as its first language are creole-speakers. Interestingly, that creole is still a pidgin for their predecessors, as in the case of Tok Pisin, or New Guinea Pidgin English (Sebba 1997: 107). Pidgin English has been in use in the Pacific islands roughly since the 1700s, and has evolved in different areas (in different socio-historical circumstances) into related pidgins. The New Guinea variety, Tok Pisin, has had a long and gradual evolution through the stabilization and expansion phases. The fact that there are over 750 indigenous languages in Papua New Guinea made Tok Pisin an indispensable lingua franca for a large percentage of the adult population and so fostered its expansion into an extended pidgin. Given its importance in such a multilingual setting, and the fact that it came to function as effectively as a 'full' language, Tok Pisin gained social prestige and was even recognized as an official language of the Republic of Papua New Guinea. However, even though it enjoyed (and still enjoys) status as a *main* language of communication, it was not until the 1960s that it became *nativized*: children began to acquire Tok Pisin as a first language. Movement of the rural populace into urban areas created families where adults with different native languages set up home together, with the result that Tok Pisin came to be used as a domestic lingua franca. Children born into such settings would therefore have become native Tok Pisin speakers and, by our definition, creole users, while their carers would have remained extended pidgin users. The same situation applies today: those who acquire Tok Pisin as a first language are classified as creole speakers, while those who use it as a language additional to their native tongues are extended pidgin users. It is important to note that the line that divides an extended pidgin from a creole is drawn on the assumption that once a language acquires native speakers, they will continue the processes of linguistic development in ways that non-native users cannot. Thus, just as many native English speakers who have used French for 25 years of their adult life will not subconsciously 'play around' and 'stretch' the rules they have consciously learnt, so too the creative faculties of extended pidgin speakers will not be put in motion in the same ways that those of all children acquiring a native language seem to be. In our New Guinea example, therefore, creole Tok Pisin should be (and, in fact, is) more linguistically complex than extended pidgin Tok Pisin.

In this discussion, we have followed a model which assumes a fairly uneventful and steady evolution from jargon → stable pidgin → extended pidgin → creole. There are, however, a couple of noteworthy points.

1 All of these stages are socially unstable, to a greater or lesser degree. The jargon of two groups in limited contact for restricted purposes is a fragile being: if that contact is withdrawn, the jargon will die. Linguistically stable pidgins too can be subject to high mortality rates: if the groups using them are broken up, for example, then they too will die. Extended pidgins and creoles, as important languages in speech communities, are more socially stable than the earlier systems but often suffer a lack of prestige. Many of them co-exist with officially recognized standard varieties of an ex-colonial language (such as standard English in the Commonwealth Caribbean); the latter of which are imbued with status and the promise of national and international social mobility. In some of these cases, extended pidgins/creoles are treated as the 'poor relations' of the official language, and are ignored in language planning strategies which instead continue to promote and confirm the authority of the standard. While extended pidgins remain a main language of communication, and creoles remain home languages which acquire successive generations of native speakers, their futures are somewhat assured; but if speakers decide against their use (most likely for reasons of prestige) then they may become susceptible to processes of **language death**.

2 The model we have used might lead us to assume that a creole, for example, necessarily evolves through each of the jargon and pidgin

stages. However, this may not be the only pathway for creole development. The socio-historical nature of the initial contact situation, and the factors that continued to shape it, appear to have resulted in different types of creoles; each of which may have followed a distinct evolutionary route. Arends *et al.* (1995: 15–17), for example, give the following creole typology, based on distinctive socio-historical contexts of formation.

> *Fort creoles*: these creoles were born in the forts set up by European traders on the West African coast. The groups in contact would have been European superstratal and African substratal speakers. The latter are likely to have been local Africans who worked for the Europeans.
>
> *Plantation creoles:* these developed through the interaction of super- and substratal speakers on New World plantations. In the Atlantic area, these groups would have been European masters and African slaves respectively, and in the Pacific, Europeans and indentured labourers from the Far East, the Philippines and the South West Pacific.
>
> *Maroon creoles*: these are creoles which may have started their lives as plantation creoles but continued to develop in marronnage, or the establishment of isolated colonies of escaped plantation slaves. Because such creoles continued to grow away from the influence of the super- and substratal speakers of the plantations, they are likely to have (a) developed new features that diverged from those of their ancestral plantation creole, and (b) preserved other features which the plantation creole would very likely lose over time, especially through increased contact with an institutionalized ex-colonial language, a phenomenon we shall explore in Chapter 3.

Hancock (1986), for instance, assumes that a type of fort creole allegedly spoken in the seventeenth century on the West African coast, Guinea Coast Creole English, developed out of a pidgin which in itself emerged from a jargon English (jargon → stable pidgin → creole). On the other hand, Bickerton (1981) hypothesizes that plantation creoles emerged in situations where there was no preceding stable, let alone expanded, pidgin phase (both of which are discussed in more detail in Chapter 2).

It is also noteworthy that differences in the physical context of development have other linguistic reflexes. Even *within* one creole type, differing circumstances of contact can produce variation

amongst it members. Take, for example, the plantation creole Berbice
Dutch (BD),[1] once the language of a Dutch-owned colony (compris-
ing plantations and small settlements) along the Berbice River, Canje
River and Wiruni Creek in Guyana (Arends *et al.* (1995: 233) state
that in 1993, there were only five remaining speakers of BD). In
1627, the Dutch Van Peere family had established a privately owned
colony on the Berbice River. Though no records about the early history of this colony have surfaced, it seems that it remained small: by
1666 it consisted of five small plantations with a total of 75 slaves.
Smith, Robertson and Williamson (1987; cited in Holm 1989: 330)
think that the majority of the slaves in the early years of the colony
spoke Eastern Ijo, an unusual occurrence (see page 5), and so needed
no other linguistic bridge amongst themselves. It is possible that
Dutch overseers learnt a rudimentary form of this substratal language in order to communicate with the slaves. On the other hand,
they may also have used a Dutch jargon which had previously been
used in trade with the indigenous Arawak Indians. In the eighteenth
century, however, the colony expanded from the initial five plantations to eight and in 1714, the Dutch West India Company shipped
in 250 slaves from Angola (Holm 1989: 331). This initiated a rapid
expansion: by 1762, Berbice had 84 private estates including 216
Europeans and 2622 African slaves (Reinecke 1937: 463; quoted in
Holm 1989). The influx of non-Eastern Ijo-speaking slaves after
1714 may have sowed the seeds of Berbice Dutch. Smith *et al.* (1987;
cited in Holm 1989) postulate that since the newcomers could not
understand Eastern Ijo, the Dutch jargon 'old slaves' may have used
in contact with their masters, became the lingua franca of the substratal community. However, the fact that Eastern Ijo was still a dominant language for this group may have meant that it played an
influential part in the evolution of this jargon into a creole.[2]

As such, BD marks plurals with a suffix *–apu*, clearly drawn from
Eastern Ijo (though for the latter, *–apu* is a plural **nominalizer** used in
the creation of 'human', as opposed to 'non-human' nouns):

Eastern Ijo (EI)
sekiapu 'dancers'; from <u>dance</u> + *–apu*
BD
kenapu 'people'; from <u>person</u> + *–apu*
emjapu 'Amy and her group'; from Amy + *–apu*

(from Arends et al. 1995: 105)

BD also marks the perfective aspect with the suffix *–te*, as in *ori* *kumte* 'he had come', which appears to have been derived from EI usage (Arends *et al.* 1995: 106). Progressive aspect is marked by the suffix *–are* (short form *–a*), as in *Kaljap, keke di wat mangimangja* 'small ones, like this one that is running up and down' (Arends *et al.* 1995: 238), which again parallels Eastern Ijo *–ari*. In addition, a large proportion of basic vocabulary items is drawn from this substratal language and not Dutch. For example, BD 'black' *kurkuru* appears to have been derived from Eastern Ijo *kurukuru*; BD *jefi* 'eat' from EI *ye fi*; and BD *jerma* 'woman' from EI *éré-me* (Arends *et al.* 1995: 234).

On the other hand, Barbados English-**lexifier** plantation creole (BEC) does not show such heavy substratal influence. The island had been made a British colony in 1624 and was initially home to tobacco plantations worked by indentured labourers, mainly from the southwestern and southern English counties of Devon, Cornwall, Somerset, Suffolk, Essex, Hertfordshire and Oxfordshire (Watts 1987: 149). Later, indentured servants came from Scotland and Ireland, particularly under Cromwell's instigation, who 'barbadosed' survivors from his campaigns in those territories. Between 1649 and 1655, Barbados received approximately 12 000 prisoners of war as indentured servants, the majority of whom were Scots and in particular, southern Irish (Watts 1987: 199).

Rickford (1986) hypothesizes that these Irish arrived in the island with little or no knowledge of English, a minority language in Ireland until the Cromwellian settlements began in the 1650s. The monolingual Irish therefore picked up the English of their co-workers from the southwestern and southern English counties, and patterns in their native Gaelic influenced the development of certain distinctive features in their English, 'in ways similar to the HE (Hiberno English) which was to become established in Ireland later' (Rickford 1986: 253).

In the latter half of the seventeenth century, the island shifted to the more lucrative cultivation of sugar, and the large-scale importation of African slaves began. However, in the early 'crossover' years, Irish servants and African slaves appear to have worked together on plantations and 'bonded' somewhat, since the former group were negatively stereotyped in the European pecking order. Cruickshank (1916: 65; cited in Rickford 1986) and Burns (1954: 39; also cited in Rickford 1986) have in fact stated that from the 1650s, Irish servants joined their African co-workers in desertion and rebellion. However, it is noteworthy that the derision shared by both ethnic groups did not automatically lead to easy intimacy. A measure of social distance was still highly likely to obtain between those whose servitude was temporary and those whose slavery lasted a lifetime. This gap no doubt increased with the size of the slave contingent, which grew rapidly: by the 1670s, Africans outnumbered Europeans by 2:1 and the ratio kept increasing. Thus, slaves may initially have had a comparatively high degree of access to the English spoken by their Irish co-workers, but not enough to result in the wholesale learning of their 'southwestern counties–Irish English'. As the slave group expanded, and doubtless came to be seen as a potential hazard, contact with Europeans (no matter how low on the social scale) decreased. The context was therefore ripe for creolization, and the product was BEC. What is distinctive about this plantation creole though, is that the effects of the initial, relatively high measure of contact with 'southwestern counties–Irish English' can still be seen. For example, habitual aspect is often expressed by *does* + main verb, as in BEC *he does write she* 'he writes to her'. This is a construction that is paralleled in Irish English (for example, *There's a sawmill here and they do take a lot of timber for palings*) and in southwestern English (as in *I do say some prayers now and again*) (Rickford 1986: 264–5). The creole also makes use of uninflected *be* in the present tense, as in *so when dem say, dem be Mr MacFlashby dey been kill, she fall back in she bed* 'so when they said that it is Mr MacFlashby that had been killed, she fell back into her bed' (Dickson 1789: 187; cited in Niles 1980: 121); a usage still found in southwestern English (as in *What be you Herb? Seventy two?* (Ihalainen 1991: 109)). BEC also retains southwestern English compounds such as *gob-stick* 'spoon', *ear-bussoms* 'tonsils', *beforetime* 'before', *left-hand-side* 'left', *sow-pig* 'sow' and *ram-sheep* 'ram' (Niles 1980).

Thus, languages such as BD and BEC demonstrate that though creoles may share certain fundamental characteristics that categorize them as a language type, they are also often individually distinctive, largely because relevant socio-historical factors differed from one creole-formation context to the next. Very often, such material was not documented, leaving modern creolists to do a fair bit of educated guesswork as to the processes that may have given rise to many of these languages. As such, the study of these areas in pidgin and creole linguistics is 'a path [which] is well trodden, but [where] the environs are untouched and little understood' (Carrington 1992: 341). The following summary to end this section may therefore help in guiding us along.

A *pidgin* is a contact language formed from the meeting of at least two mutually unintelligible systems. It may begin life as a secondary hybrid or jargon created primarily for specific types of communication (such as trade) between groups that already have native languages. However, if a group decides that this jargon should be extended beyond its original purpose, a process of tertiary hybridization (which results in *stablization*) can occur, turning it into a linguistically stable but impoverished (that is, reduced in structure) pidgin. A pidgin may further undergo an *expansion* phase, which results in a more complex extended pidgin. Though a pidgin can be a main language of communication, it is never a native language since it is used by adults that already have mother tongues. However, if it is taken on (at any developmental stage) as a first language by those born into a pidgin-speaking community, and who inevitably continue its linguistic and social evolution, it becomes *nativized* into a *creole*.

Note, though, the possibility that a creole can quickly arise without a prior stable pidgin phase. Creoles have the structural complexity of 'full' languages yet are often granted comparatively low social status, even by their native speakers. Thus, even though they can theoretically be used in areas that carry high social status (such as government, education, literature), efforts to develop and utilize them in such ways do not always meet with widespread support.

We can now turn our attention to other linguistic environs that the pidgin and creole path cuts through.

1.3 Pidgins and creoles in linguistics

In the nineteenth century, Schuchardt, 'the father of creole studies' (Holm 1988: 29) stated that 'the importance for general linguistics of the creole dialects has not yet been fully appreciated'.[3] Creoles first came to notice in the seventeenth century, a time of overseas colonial and commercial expansion for Europe. The first known observation of a creole was recorded in 1685 by Le Courbe, a French navigator:

> These Sengalese, besides the language of the country also speak a certain jargon which resembles but little the Portuguese language and which is called the creole language

> (Cited by Chaudenson 1979: 9; quoted in Holm 1988: 15)

During this early period of contact, creoles were of interest only insofar as they could be of practical use – they were indispensable to Europeans in establishing trade, outposts, colonies and in attempts at religious conversion. Word and phrase lists (with translations) of various creoles were therefore compiled, sometimes accompanied by explorers' and travellers' thoughts about the origins of these languages and their uses. For example, Père Chévillard, a priest in Martinique, commented in his manuscript that the African slaves there were 'attentive observers who rapidly familiarised themselves with the language of the European, which was purposely corrupted to facilitate its comprehension' (in Holm 1988: 16). Observations such as these constituted the embryonic stages of the explicit condemnation that would later be directed towards creoles and their speakers. In them also lay the seeds of the derogatory terminology, such as *broken English, bastard Portuguese, nigger French,* that would later be applied to creoles, and cemented in the minds of many of their native speakers.

Detailed investigation into creoles did not begin until the 1730s, when Moravian missionaries attempted to convert slaves on the island of Saint Thomas and in Suriname by using the latter's Dutch-lexifier creole. They taught the slaves to read and write in this language and produced an abundance of grammars, dictionaries and translations of the gospels, sermons and songs. At first glance, such undertakings may seem to have been the result of enlightened thinking, given that they occurred simultaneously with the extensive **linguistic prescriptivism** that was sweeping through Europe. However, as progressive as the Moravians now appear, it is likely that their decision to conduct ecclesiastical business in the creole was largely a necessary acquiescence to facilitate their mission. Thus, missionaries such as Oldendorp (1777) wrote that the creole he used in his work was 'a mutilation without plan or rule' (in Holm 1988: 19).

The rest of the eighteenth and early nineteenth centuries brought increasing interest, scholarly and otherwise, in creole languages. Thus, in 1780 the Dutch published the first grammar and dictionary of Malayo-Portuguese and in 1802, a guide book to Haiti was compiled, complete with creole conversations and, for the first time, a French ↔ French-lexifier creole vocabulary to help the unseasoned traveller get by. However, increased interest in and knowledge of creoles did not engender unbiased, or at least more tolerant, views of these languages generally. For example, in 1829 the British and Foreign Bible Society in London published the first complete edition of *Da Njoe Testament* in Sranan, a Surinamese creole, for the Moravians. The founder of an Edinburgh newspaper was aghast that 'the broken English of the Negroes', as he put it, had now been permanently encoded in the written (not to mention holy, in this case) medium and that it would be but a short step to incorporating their 'blundering phraseology', 'their barbarous, mixed, imperfect phrase in the pages of schoolbooks' (Holm 1988: 21). Such outbursts did not pass unchecked. For example, the philologist William Greenfield responded that the linguistic processes that result in creoles and other full languages are identical and that 'the Negroes have been proved to be in no degree inferior to other nations' (Greenfield 1830: 48–51; quoted in Holm 1988: 22). However, the overwhelming perception of the time in European societies that participated in the slave trade was that the Africans were a biologically and culturally inferior race, and by extension, so were their creoles:

> It is clear that people used to expressing themselves with a rather simple language cannot easily elevate their intelligence to the genius of a European language. When they were in contact with the Portuguese and forced to communicate with them . . . it was necessary that the varied expressions acquired during so many centuries of civilisation dropped their perfection, to adapt to ideas being born and to barbarous forms of language of half-savage peoples.
>
> (Bertrand-Bocandé 1849: 73, on Guinean Creole Portuguese; cited in Holm 1988: 22–23)

This type of notion persisted throughout the work of many nineteenth-century scholars. Even though academics such as Schuchardt, Van Name, Coelho and Meillet (see Holm 1988: Chapter 2) did much to raise the profile of creoles as languages of interest to linguists, the cultural perspectives of their time inevitably infiltrated their work. For example, Schuchardt (1887: 138; in Holm 1988: 23) suggested that the predominance of **labialized** sounds in the Portuguese-lexifier creole of Cape Verde 'can be explained by the well developed lips of the Negroes'.

Nevertheless, the work of such linguists established the foundations of significant enquiry into the nature of creole languages. They addressed, among others, questions of creole genesis, the social nature of language contact and of language mixing: issues that we shall be exploring in more detail. In so doing, they introduced pidgins and creoles into the world of general linguistics, where they have provided points of interest and controversy ever since.

In 1974, Bickerton wrote that 'creole studies has a unique opportunity of contributing to, perhaps even decisively influencing, the

development of general linguistics – an opportunity foreseen by
Schuchardt nearly a century ago' (1974: 85). Even though pidgins
and creoles are now studied extensively, there had initially been a
measure of reluctance in some quarters in incorporating them into
other established theories of language perhaps because, as
Mühlhäusler (1986: 275) points out, they question certain fundamental assumptions in these areas. Justification for ignoring these
challenges came from the view of pidgins and creoles as atypical; in
other words, as systems that have their genesis in aberrant circumstances. They were therefore often dismissed as 'freak case[s] for
whose sake a general theory of language should not be changed'
(Mühlhäusler 1986).

Yet, the very existence of these 'freak cases' argued for their inclu-
sion into wider linguistic theory. Twentieth-century linguistics generally aims to be descriptive and, as such, there was an increasing
awareness that pidgins and creoles should not be proscribed by the
assumption that they are too exceptional to be incorporated into the
rule. Therefore, areas of enquiry such as historical linguistics, sociolinguistics and psycholinguistics (each of which aims to describe linguistic behaviour and which, together, can build a three-dimensional
picture of language use) are paying renewed attention to the data
emerging from the field of creolistics. In the following sections, we
will look at some of the areas where creole studies has made or is
making an impact.

1.3.1 Sociolinguistics

Sociolinguistics is an area of enquiry which has not been slow in taking account of pidgins and creoles, perhaps because the latter are clear
proof that an in-depth understanding of how a communication system works is impossible without an examination of its social context.
It might seem common sense to suppose that no such 'proof' is
required, but for a long time, as Sebba (1997: 288–9) points out, the
dominant schools of linguistic thought (**structuralist** and **generative
linguistics**) analysed languages as static objects and treated the social
aspects of their use as marginal. Pidgins and creoles have served as
useful 'living labs' in overturning this view because, as we have seen,
they are systems which result from particular social circumstances that
necessitate communication between culturally and linguistically
diverse speakers. Many also continue to exist in multilingual and

multicultural societies, as in Trinidad (an island in the southerly Caribbean) where an English-lexifier creole (**TEC**) is currently the mother tongue of a population that comprises people of African, East Indian, Chinese, Portuguese, French, Spanish, Syrian-Lebanese and Amerinidian (to name a few!) ancestries. There are still areas, such as Paramín (a remote mountain-top village formed in the eighteenth century by runaway slaves), where an older, French-lexifier, maroon creole (TFC) is spoken, albeit alongside TEC. Two generations ago, TEC also co-existed with Bhojpuri, the first language of the majority of the East Indian immigrants (still spoken or understood by many Trinidadian East Indians). Such a multilingual setting has impacted on the development of TEC, which now shows influence from Bhojpuri (largely in the area of lexis) and TFC. Examples like these therefore show that any worthwhile analysis of such languages must take account of their individual social contexts, in both **synchronic** and **diachronic** dimensions. Thus, the study of pidgins and creoles has generally lent weight to the sociolinguistic enterprise because they, very simply, remind linguists of the basic fact that 'without people interacting in a context, there can be no language' (Sebba 1997: 288–9).

One of the more specific issues on which pidgins and creoles have impacted is that of language transmission. It has generally been assumed that the 'handing down' of a language from generation to generation takes place smoothly in a stable speech community. Thus, even though the usage of each generation may necessarily come to include features that distinguish it from the last, they all still essentially speak the same language, since the social coherence of the speech community ensures an uneventful and gradual evolution. Thus Labov (1972: 120) famously defined the speech community as an entity 'not defined by any marked agreement in the use of language elements, so much as by participation in shared norms'. It would seem, however, that social instability may have been a defining feature of the environments that produced pidgins and creoles. Take, for example, the typical plantation context, home to a pidgin-using substratal group. The composition of the group was constantly open to fluctuation: large numbers of new slaves (and therefore new substratal speakers) were brought in, while some were lost through marronnage (see page 9 of this volume), manumission (or the purchase of freedom) or disease. In addition, plantations sometimes changed hands, which could mean the imposition of a new superstratal variety, or in cases of wider social upheavals, a new superstratal language. Thus, if the configuration of the pidgin-using community was in constant flux, then so too would be the use of the pidgin, which would then seem to be in a continuous state of being re-defined.

Despite this changeable nature, stable and extended pidgins and creoles quickly and variously evolved, not over the course of several generations but sometimes, it would seem, within the space of one or two. In fact, as stated in Section 1.2, it has been hypothesized that certain creoles may have come into being before their predecessor pidgins had had time to stabilize. Because of such possibilities, sociolinguistics now distinguishes between gradual or *normal transmission* and *abnormal transmission*, the latter of which would seem to be a defining feature of many socially unstable pidgin → creole-speaking communities. Abnormal transmission also covers cases of *abrupt creolization*, 'where a creole arises without a preceding stable pidgin, through a sharp break in the transmission of language in some community' (Sebba 1997: 136). An example of such discontinuity in transmission can possibly be seen in the social context that produced Mauritian Creole. The Indian Ocean island was discovered by the Portuguese in the sixteenth century, settled by the Dutch in the seventeenth, and abandoned by the latter but claimed by the French in the eighteenth. From 1715 onwards, French settlers (including some from the neighbouring French island colony of Réunion) imported slaves from Madagascar, West and East Africa, and India. The proportion of slaves rapidly outstripped that of Europeans from 1727 onwards and, by 1777, mention was being made of a local creole. The island was captured by the British in the Napoleonic wars and English became the official language. However, French remained the language of a small elite and Mauritian Creole (MC) that of the bulk of the population. Chaudenson (1974) suggested that MC was a local development of the creole of Réunion, transposed by the migrants from that island. However, Baker and Corne (1982) have countered on the basis of historical data that MC developed in the island very rapidly (between 1727–38) without a prior stable pidgin phase. According to parish registers, 465 children were born to slave mothers in this period. It is these children who, in Baker and Corne's hypothesis, nativized a form that had not yet had time to stabilize and expand. If they are correct, then MC may be a case of abrupt creolization, where there has been a huge leap (not gradual transmission) between the linguistic usage of one generation and the next. Instances such as these therefore suggest that for some languages, 'the whole linear notion of gradual change' may 'not even [be] a superficially useful approximation to the truth' (Hoenigswald 1971: 476; quoted in Mühlhäusler 1986: 256).

Looking at how linguistic variation and change occur in creole-speaking communities has also been useful in highlighting the role of the individual speaker and the social factors that affect their language use. Le Page and Tabouret-Keller (1985: 1) state that sociolinguistics has traditionally located processes of variation (and, as we saw earlier, language transmission and change) in the speech community; it starts 'from the supposition that there are languages in the use of which members of a community vary ... "languages" and "groups" have been taken as given, the starting points'. They believe, however, that the real fountainhead is the individual, since it is the latter that comprises each building block of the group: concepts such as 'sharing a language' and 'belonging to a community' 'come into being through the acts of identity which people make within themselves and each other'. In fact, 'groups or communities and the linguistic attributes of such groups have no existential locus other than in the minds of individuals ... and [they] inhere only in the way individuals behave towards each other' (Le Page and Tabouret-Keller 1985: 4–5). This sentiment is present in earlier work, such as Le Page (1968) which suggests that:

> Each individual creates the system for his verbal behaviour so that they shall resemble those of the group or groups with which from time to time he may wish to be identified, to the extent that
> a he can identify the groups,
> b he has both opportunity and ability to observe and analyse their behavioural systems,
> c his motivation is sufficiently strong to impel him to choose, and to adapt his behaviour accordingly,
> d he is still able to adapt his behaviour.

One of the most famous models of variation in creole-speaking communities, DeCamp's (1971) *creole continuum* (discussed in Chapter 3), builds on this premise. DeCamp proposed that in communities where a creole co-exists with the standard variety of its original superstratal language or *lexifier*, a range of varieties that mix the two evolve. The hypothesis states that many creole speakers are united in viewing acquisition of the standard as desirable, but as *individuals,* will have differing levels of access to it, because of factors such as 'age, poverty, and isolation from urban centers' (DeCamp 1971: 351). The result of this is a range of mixed lects that resemble either the creole or the standard to a greater or lesser degree. In addition, some creole speakers consciously reject acquisition of the standard and embrace instead the creole. In DeCamp's words, 'acculturative influences impinge on *different speakers* with varying degrees of effectiveness, drawing some of them more than others towards the standard' (1971: 351). In such situations, therefore, the linguistic decisions made by the individual, as far as he or she was able, are important in understanding language use.

The continuum model has mainly been applied only to creole-speaking communities and, indeed, not all creolists agree that it is the most adequate means of describing the variation found there (see Chapter 3). Nevertheless, it has aided in emphasizing the fact that such phenomena cannot effectively be studied or understood without focusing on the actual people in a community and on the various social factors that determine where they, as individuals, position themselves, at any given time, in 'linguistic space'.

It is noteworthy that the study of pidgins and creoles has benefited in turn from sociolinguistic research and methods. Winford (1997: 305) mentions for example that creolists are paying 'increased attention' to factors that sociolinguistics has established as being integral to an understanding of language use; factors such as 'demographics, community settings and codes of social interaction'. Creolists have also turned their attention to raising the profile of creoles in their speech communities and maximizing their potential, thus drawing on models set in the area of applied sociolinguistics. As such, there is an increasing body of research into methods (and problems) of effectively integrating creoles into educational and public life, as well as into related issues such as achieving standardization (see Chapter 4 for a more detailed discussion). In addition, scholars are looking at sociolinguistic phenomena such as miscommunication and gendered usage in creole interaction and applying, where relevant, the techniques of discourse analysis. As such, pidgins and creoles may be on their way to realizing their 'full potential to contribute much to our understanding of the relationship between language and social life' (Winford 1997: 314).

1.3.2 Historical linguistics

Unlike much of the work of sociolinguistics, which is based on contemporary data, the study of diachronic processes that affect, and have affected, linguistic evolution and change is often necessarily confined to theoretical abstraction. It is, for example, practically impossible to thoroughly investigate developments in a language that once existed 3000 years ago. In addition, because processes of change often occur very slowly through time, working out what they may have been, what may have catalysed them and what they might have resulted in, can be a monumental and labour-intensive task for the historical linguist who, very often, formulates hypotheses based solely on textual materials (sometimes limited in number) written by long-dead speakers. However, pidgins and creoles, which are comparatively new systems that undergo change fairly rapidly, theoretically bring us as close as possible to observing language genesis and change in progress. As McMahon (1994: 265) points out, theories that have been formulated to this end in historical linguistics but which are difficult to test 'can be directly observed or at least recovered in pidgins and creoles ... [which] may allow for confirmation [or rejection!] of various hypotheses'.

It was in the context of this 'lab value' of pidgins and creoles that Mühlhäusler (1986: 252) first asserted that data from these languages present a challenge to 'certain views of language history and relationships, in particular the view that languages are genetically related to a single ancestral language'. This idea of 'linguistic relatedness', fundamental to the majority of research in historical linguistics, first took shape in the work of Sir William Jones, an eighteenth-century philologer and lawyer in the British foreign service. In the course of a posting in India, during which time he worked with ancient legal documents written in Sanskrit, Jones realized that quite a few of its lexical items bore a striking resemblance to those in classical Latin and Greek. Thus, the Sanskrit *pitar* 'father' was **cognate** with the Latin and Greek *pater*; Sanskrit *matar* 'mother' with Latin *mater* and Greek *meter*; and *naktam* 'night' with *noctis* and *nuktos*. Since it was unlikely that these languages had ever been in a situation of contact with each other (which would have facilitated a borrowing of these terms), such similarities, in Jones's view, were due to something much more remarkable. On the basis of his comparisons, Jones proposed to the Asiatick Society in Calcutta the one-time existence of a 'common source', since these three languages shared 'a stronger affinity ... than could possibly have been produced by accident; so strong, indeed, that no philologer could examine them all three, without believing them to have sprung from some common source, which perhaps, no longer exists' (Jones 1786; quoted in McCrum *et al.* 1992: 47).

Later work only served to strengthen this proposition. Historical linguists undertook **comparative** and **internal reconstruction**, based on two main principles:

1 that languages comprise 'stable' and 'unstable' elements, and
2 that certain types of change in language are internally motivated (that is, not caused by language contact but by 'growth' processes intrinsic to the development of the language); these changes are therefore regular and rule-governed.

Fundamental components of a language's grammatical system, such as its **morphosyntax**, were considered stable elements, since it was believed that they remained largely unaffected in language contact situations; while an 'unstable' component such as the lexicon was open to outside influence (that is, was susceptible to borrowing). There was, however, a measure of overlap between the two elements, since languages possess what came to be known as *core vocabularies*: a supposedly stable component of the lexicon which names concepts common to human experience and as such includes pronouns, kinship terms and those that label the physically universal environment (concepts such as 'night', 'day', 'sun' and 'moon'). It was assumed that core vocabularies would also be impervious in language contact situations, since there would be no need for the speakers involved to borrow terminology for 'basic' concepts which they had already identified and named.

Traditional historical linguistics therefore hypothesized that if two languages, A and B, came into contact, neither's morphosyntax and core vocabulary would change as a direct result since they were 'systèmes fermés', 'closed systems' (Meillet 1967: 84). However, an unstable component, such as the majority of the lexicon, would. The outcome of such contact would therefore be a case of lexical borrowing: A and/or B might take on lexical items from the other's vocabulary stock, but their individual 'linguistic essence' would remain untouched. Any developments that could be seen to have occurred in these 'closed systems' were accordingly assumed to be the result of internal workings. As such, language contact, in affecting only vocabulary, was considered an insignificant factor in causing language change.

Internal processes of change, as stated in point (2) above, were thought to be regular, rule-governed and, as such, to generate predictable results. The consequences of this theory are twofold. First, this means that grammatical processes occurring at one stage of a language's life can provide clues (if you know the rules!) to earlier processes. You can therefore work backwards with data from one language, internally reconstructing its past stages. Second, the idea that stable elements exist and do not change because of language contact means that if different languages have similar grammatical systems and core vocabularies, then they are similar not because of borrowing but because these languages *must* be related. Such languages can therefore be grouped into families, and correspondences among their stable elements, or core, used to carry out comparative reconstruction of earlier stages of each, and also of earlier linguistic ancestors.

The comparative method of reconstruction makes use of a family tree model, much like that we use to trace and represent our genealogy, to represent these relationships. The linguistic version, however, recognizes only one ancestor at each level, thus codifying the assumed unimportance of language contact in tracing 'essential' linguistic development, which occurs through internal transmission from *mother language* to *daughter languages*. Thus, as can be seen in Figure 1.1, the stable elements of contemporary languages such as English and Frisian are similar enough for them to be classified as sisters. Comparative work has reconstructed their mother, Anglo-Frisian, which in turn is a sister language of Netherlandic-Germanic. Data from the latter two sisters and their mother, West Germanic, along with that from various *cousins*, have helped in the comparative reconstruction of their mother, Germanic, and of Proto-Indo-European, the latter of which is held to be the progenitor of many of the languages of Europe and Asia.

This method of representation, and the processes that generate it, have long been established in linguistics. Yet, for some scholars, it is but a 'cultural interpretation ... rather than [an] objective mirror of reality' (Mühlhäusler 1986: 252). For example, it is arguable that the linguistic family tree is only as real as the assumption that languages have stable elements that are not vulnerable to change in situations of contact. But what if this is in fact not the case? It is well known, for example, that when the early stage of English known as Anglo-Saxon came into sustained contact with Old Norse (a related dialect) as a result of the ninth-century Danelaw settlement, 'unpredictable' changes occurred in its grammar and core vocabulary. Thus Anglo-Saxon borrowed the Norse pronoun forms *they, them, their* replacing *he, hem* and *heora*, as well as other basic vocabulary items such as *sister, husband, egg* and *ugly*. It has also been argued that the loss of inflections marking **case** and of **grammatical gender** in Anglo-

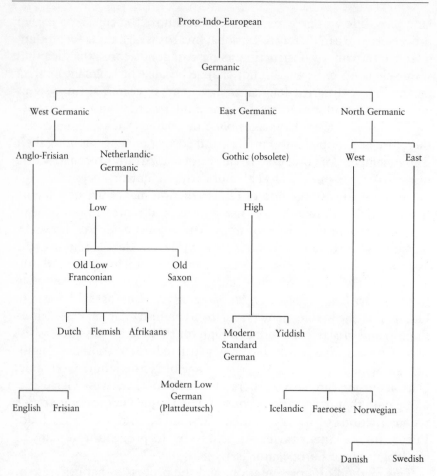

Figure 1.1 The Germanic branch of the Proto-Indo-European tree

Saxon may have been caused by contact with Old Norse. A similar hypothesis has been that the later co-existence of English with Norman French for approximately 200 years after the Conquest also contributed to many of the grammatical changes that occurred in the Middle English Period (1100–1500). Thus, it may be that prolonged and sustained contact can affect more than elements of a language's vocabulary.

Such well-documented instances have not, however, engendered any re-thinking of the family tree model, since it can be argued, for instance, that the core borrowings from Old Norse were in fact minimal, and that the grammatical changes that occurred in English during the respective contact periods with Old Norse and Norman French were already under way, as part of the regular processes that characterize the movement from a highly **synthetic** to an **analytic** grammar. In addition, at no point did the contact between English and Old Norse, or English and Norman French, produce an entirely new language. In other words, English continued to be English. In the light of this, there is therefore no need to represent such periods of contact on a linguistic family tree. Similarly, though we do not know beyond a shadow of a doubt that a language such as East Germanic was the sole progenitor of Gothic, we assume, for the purpose of the model and the method of reconstruction on which it was based, that it was. The model therefore reflects and reinforces the idea that 'established' languages are not the product of language contact but of gradual, 'genetically asexual' evolution.

An inevitable consequence of this was the idea that if stable elements were somehow severely breached in a contact situation, the result would be a linguistic mutant – a language that combined, for example, many of the morphosyntactic features of both parents. Nineteenth-century scholars, often heavily influenced by theological notions on the desirable state of purity in all things (cf. Douglas 1996) found this possibility unsettling: 'such a thing as a language with a mixed grammatical apparatus has never come under the cognizance of linguistic students: It would be to them a monstrosity; it seems an impossibility' (Whitney 1867: 199; quoted in Farrar 1996).

Given, then, this belief that languages are classifiable only in rela-tion to one ancestor at a time, how were pidgins and creoles to be dealt with, given that they have at least two progenitor language groups in their genealogy: the superstratum and the superstrata? Were they therefore living proof that language contact was not as insignificant as previously thought?

Schuchardt, who believed that all languages had, at some point in their history, undergone significant changes even in their core because of language contact (*Es gibt keine völlig ungemischte Sprache* 'there are no completely unmixed languages'), thought that they were. However, many of his contemporaries (and indeed, later scholars) refuted this, preferring instead to make languages such as pidgins and creoles 'fit' the existing framework, either by assuming that they were aberrant exceptions to the rule (Mühlhäusler's 'freak cases') or that they were in fact essentially descendants of one parent and not two.

Thus, the nineteenth-century scholar Meillet asserted, in reaction to Schuchardt, that pidgins and creoles were descendants of their superstratal languages (that is, they inherited grammatical components such as their morphosyntax and core vocabularies from this parent) which had undergone limited lexical borrowing from the substrata. They could therefore be classified with a superstratal parent, a conclusion which safeguarded the linguistic family tree model:

> If we have been able to succeed in reconstructing the history of some languages by comparison, it is because we were sure that each new system had to be explained as coming from a single system. In the case where one would have to take account of two initial systems and of their reactions to each other, the present methods would not be sufficient ... *In spite of the hypotheses made in this direction, linguists have, fortunately, never yet been surely in the face of such a difficulty.*

> (1967: 102; quoted in Holm 1988: 34; emphasis mine)

Twentieth-century creolists also subscribed, at least in part, to Meillet's opinion. Even though Hall in 1966, for example, conceded the possibility of borrowing taking place in the purported stable elements, he defended the family tree model as suitable for the genetic classification of pidgins and creoles on the grounds that, again, the latter were essentially a continuation of their respective superstratal languages with comparatively limited borrowings from their substrata:

> But even though all languages are 'mixed', some – to paraphrase Orwell's famous expression – are more 'mixed' than others. We are left with the question whether, in fact, the more mixed languages are so mixed as to invalidate the assumption of genetic relationship, particularly as applied to languages of whose history we have no detailed knowledge. In theory, a language might conceivably combine elements from two or more sources so that they were perfectly evenly balanced and so that they would be, therefore, unclassifiable according to our customary assumption. *Yet, in practice, such a condition of perfect balance is never found – not even in any of the pidgins and creoles that have been investigated ... and not even with their (admittedly extensive) carry-overs, in structure as well as vocabulary, from [their] substrata.* In Haitian Creole, the proportion of French structure is both greater and more fundamental than

that of African-type structure; and the same is true of Chinese Pidgin English, Neo-Melanesian, Sranan, Gullah etc., in relation to English and the various substrata involved.

(Hall 1966: 117; emphasis mine)

Incidentally, this perspective would seem to underlie frequently used labels such as *English-based pidgin* or *Spanish-based creole*, which imply the dominance of superstratal structure.

Conversely, other creolists have argued for the provenance of the substratal parent in pidgin and creole classification. Given that in many cases the bulk of a pidgin's and creole's lexis appears to be derived from the superstratal parent (hence more recent labels such as *English-lexifier pidgin/creole*), the theory here is that pidgins and creoles combine this with a substratal grammatical (and perhaps even a core lexical) inheritance. Thus, Suzanne Sylvain, for example, writing on Haiti's French-lexifier creole (which, as we saw above, was categorized by Hall as a daughter of French!) stated that:

We are in the presence of French cast in the mold of African syntax or, since languages are classed according to their syntax, an Ewe language with French vocabulary.

(1936: 178; quoted in Holm 1988: 37)

Such a conclusion would initially seem to point to a relatively unproblematic categorization of such a creole: it goes on the family tree of its African parent. At the same time, however, it raises some interesting questions. For example, while the traditional idea of contact allows for either limited, moderate or even abundant lexical borrowing between languages, it does not cater for the wholesale replacement of one vocabulary stock by another (as Sylvain implies Ewe has done with French), which constitutes a huge structural change. It could be argued that Sylvain's hypothesis does not resolve the classification debate but instead blurs it even further. Intuitively, we may feel that what we have here is an entirely new language – it is not really Ewe, since the vocabulary is French; neither is it French, since the grammar is Ewe. Thus, can it truly be classified with Ewe on a tree that will, by its very nature, show no contact with French?

The label *mixed language* came to be applied in such cases. Mixture implied not that a creole's grammatical system, for example, was a fusion of features inherited from both parents but instead, in keeping with the old idea that grammars were still largely impenetrable

in contact situations, referred to the sandwiching together of components as described by Sylvain:

> A very rough approximation is that a mixed language has its
> lexicon and grammar from different sources. On the basis of the
> lexicon one would classify such languages as belonging to one
> language family and on the basis of the morphology, syntax and
> general grammatical characteristics one would classify them as
> belonging to another language family.

> (Bakker and Mous 1994: 5)

Taylor (1956: 413; quoted in McMahon 1994: 269) suggested that
creoles could therefore be labelled genetic 'orphans' which had two
'foster-parents', providing grammar and lexicon respectively.
Keeping and extending the family metaphor in such a way was, however, still problematic since, apart from the fact that the terminology
immediately marked out pidgins and creoles as atypical (and at worst
deviant) members of 'linguistic society', the traditional linguistic
family tree had no room for 'foster-parents' and 'orphans', simply
because it was not set up to accommodate that mode of representation.

Establishing a new family tree would not necessarily have solved
the problem either. For example, many creoles which have not, as far
as we know, been in contact with each other at any point in their history, share certain structural similarities. This has therefore been
taken to indicate, in the context of Jones' work (see page 21 of this
volume), that these too must have sprung from a common source, a
proto-pidgin (an idea explored in the theory of monogenesis, see
Chapter 2). This could mean the creation of a new family tree, with
a head 'mother pidgin', from whom a network of daughters, sisters
and cousins emanate. However, such a tree could still cause more
problems than it solved. For example, monogeneticists have proposed that a plausible proto-pidgin, combining a superstratally
derived lexicon with a grammatical system inherited from the substrata, was one formed on the West African coast through contact
between Portuguese and West African slave traders: West African
Pidgin Portuguese (WAPP). When speakers of this Portuguese-lexifier
pidgin (primarily slaves, who learnt it while in captivity on the
African coast), found themselves in various New World territories,
such as English-, French- or Dutch-owned plantations, they
relexified, or exchanged word for word, their Portuguese-derived

conclusion

vocabulary for that which was dominant in their respective environments. However, the proto-pidgin's West African grammatical core was retained in each daughter, meaning that the latter could therefore neatly be classified with their mother-pidgin in a creole family tree. Yet, even here problems arise. If the tree, theoretically modelled as it is on its more established counterpart, only allows for one ancestor at any one level, then the different 'relexifier parents', obviously a significant factor in each creole's make-up, cannot be represented. If the individual native languages of proto-pidgin-speaking slaves 'interfered' with their usage of the latter (a common occurrence in the acquisition and use of a non-native second language), and caused structural changes in the pidgin, then that too cannot be accounted for. Furthermore, we eventually end up at a familiar question: Where do we place WAPP itself? Is the proto-pidgin to be classified with Portuguese in the Indo-European tree, or with one or more West African languages in the **Hamitic** tree, or is it a genetic orphan derived from both trees?

basically it doesn't work

Some linguists have therefore moved away from trying to fit pidgins and creoles into a model that cannot satisfactorily account for them. Thomason and Kaufman (1988: 10; 11), for example, agree that pidgins and creoles are mixed in the sense defined by Sylvain and by later scholars such as Bakker and Mous but argue that this is inadequate justification for classifying them with their grammatical (substratal) parent. In their view, similarities between the stable elements of languages are not enough to warrant a label of genetic relationship. This instead necessitates 'systematic correspondences in *all* parts of the language because that is what results from *normal* transmission: what is transmitted is an entire language – that is, a complex set of interrelated lexical, phonological, morphosyntactic, and semantic structures' (Thomason and Kaufman 1988: 11; emphasis mine). Thus in a case of abnormal transmission that results in a creole, for example (see Section 1.3.1), no one 'whole' language is inherited by one generation from another. In addition, the speakers of this mixed language system will also evolve features that are exclusively its own (see Section 1.2). A creole does not therefore 'belong' to either its superstratum or substrata. It is in fact a 'non-genetic' language, which renders it unclassifiable:

> pidgins and creoles ... do not fit within the genetic model and therefore cannot be classified at all ... we do not believe that a creole can reasonably be viewed as a changed later form of its

vocabulary-base language; there is, in fact, no language that has changed. Instead, an entirely new language – without genetic affiliation – is created by the first members of the multilingual community, and further developed and stabilized by later members.

(Thomason and Kaufman 1988: 3, 165–6)

The authors also make the point that such non-genetic languages are not unusual, citing for example the case of Ma'a, a language spoken in Tanzania. In terms of genetic classification, Ma'a had originally been categorized as a Cushitic language. Today it retains about 50 per cent Cushitic vocabulary (including its core lexis) and a few Cushitic grammatical elements, but has borrowed the rest of its structure from Bantu, a language with which it has been in sustained contact. Thus, in direct contradiction to traditional assumptions, a great deal of Ma'a's morphosyntactic (as well as phonological) features comprise borrowings from Bantu. For example Ma'a, like Cushitic, used to have SOV word order and make use of post-positions, but now, in line with Bantu, it uses SVO order and prepositions (McMahon 1994: 212). Therefore Ma'a is now arguably neither Cushitic nor Bantu (though Mous (1994; cited in Sebba 1997: 266) does not agree with this analysis; see Sebba 1997: 265–6), any more than an individual is structurally more of her mother than her father, or vice versa.

In summary, languages such as Ma'a, pidgins and creoles would seem to be living testimony to the fact that languages can be structurally indebted to more than one ancestor. However, whether they challenge the *viability* of the established 'single-ancestor' model is arguable. As Thomason and Kaufman (1988: 3) point out, that mixed languages exist does not negate the fact that unmixed ones are highly likely to as well, and the genetic model creates an effective grouping for the latter. What historical linguistics has taken on board from pidgin and creole research is the fact that the results of language contact can be more far-reaching than lexical borrowing; and that the *social context* of that contact, which may result in normal or abnormal transmission, for instance, is important in determining the linguistic outcome. In so doing, pidgin and creole data have aided in linking the findings of socio- and historical linguistics: a desirable state of affairs for a field that is generally concerned with questions of linguistic evolution and change; and an apt role for bridging languages!

Another area in historical linguistics where pidgin and creole data has come to be considered is in debates about what constitutes *naturalness* in linguistic systems. In its broadest sense, the term *natural* has traditionally been applied to languages such as English or Hindi vis-à-vis man-made constructs such as Esperanto or computer languages. The former are *natural* insofar as 'their rules and conventions are mainly unconscious and, it is argued, are not directly amenable to human interference' (Mühlhäusler 1986: 60–1).

More specifically, *naturalness* has been defined in the area of language change in terms of *markedness*. To understand this fully, we need to go back to the concept of genetic affiliation between languages. If languages are in fact genetically related, then there is a 'linguistic DNA' that holds between them. For example, if language C is the mother of language D, then just as (ignoring the existence of fathers for the moment!) a human mother passes on some of her traits to her daughter, so too will D inherit characteristics from C. These inheritances are, in both instances, genetically determined (i.e. inbuilt into the 'biology' of transmission) and are therefore *natural* or *unmarked*. However, if a human daughter were to acquire a permanent scar from an accident, for example, then that new feature of her make-up would be non-genetic, non-naturally acquired and therefore *marked*. Similarly, if language D was to come into contact with another, it is possible that they might acquire or borrow features from each other (see above) which they would not otherwise have had and which therefore would also be *marked*.

This definition of *naturalness* has been applied to pidgins, with particular reference to phonological and grammatical properties, such as the preference for **CVCV** (Consonant Vowel) structure and a lack of tonal distinctions; as well as the lack of a passive voice and of overt plural marking. It is not difficult to see why: we too may instinctively feel that such features are in a sense more 'basic', or *natural* in languages. For example, it may be universally easier to pronounce CVCV structures than consonant clusters and to make semantic distinctions by means other than changes in tone (as in, for example, Mandarin Chinese where *mā* (level tone) means 'mother', but *má* (rising tone) an indigenous plant used in clothes making; *mǎ* (fall-rise tone) 'horse' and *mà* (falling tone) 'abuse'$_{verb}$). Similarly, the category of 'one' is likely to universally precede that of 'more than one'; hence the singular is the base, *natural* or *unmarked* form. The active voice (which allows for transparent agent+action+affected structures; as in *the dog*$_{agent}$ *bit*$_{action}$ *the baby*$_{affected}$), also seems more

elemental than its related but potentially opaque passive voice (where
the affected is foregrounded and the agent is not obligatory; as in *the
baby*_{affected} *was bitten*_{action} *[by the dog]*_{agent}). By definition, since creoles
will develop more complex structures, such as plural marking and
passive structures, they therefore come to adopt *non-natural* or
marked solutions, like many other long-established languages.

Trudgill (1983), in defining the changes typically found in situations of pidginization and creolization, challenged this categorization
of *natural* and *non-natural*. He stated that *natural* changes are those
which are likely to occur in all linguistic systems, not because of
external factors (such as contact with another language) but because
of 'the inherent nature of the linguistic systems themselves' (Trudgill
1983; quoted in McMahon 1994: 266). *Non-natural* changes therefore, were those which occurred in situations of language contact.
Trudgill defined processes such as **grammaticalization** and **assimilation** as *natural* and others, such as reduced use of inflected forms,
increased use of prepositions and the development of fixed word
order, as *non-natural*. Features such as the latter are in fact typical of
pidgins, and as they develop in situations of contact, they can therefore be classified, in this framework, as *non-natural* systems. The definitions, however, become somewhat problematic with regard to
creoles. Creoles do exhibit changes such as grammaticalization and
assimilation: features of *natural* languages. Yet to classify creoles as
natural is to erroneously imply, first, that they have not developed out
of situations of contact and, second, to ignore the fact that many creoles co-exist (and therefore maintain a situation of contact) with
other languages. In addition, Trudgill suggested that *natural* changes
tend to take place more slowly than those that are *non-natural*.
However, as stated in Section 1.2.1, creoles tend to develop at an
accelerated rate, sometimes undergoing expansion and elaboration in
a single generation. A further complication arises in that there may
be cases where it is difficult to differentiate between a *natural* and
non-natural process. For example, let us assume that Language A
and Language B are in contact. Language A begins to undergo a
process of grammaticalization that will turn a full verb into a verbal
suffix (as in *tu* <u>*has*</u> 'you have' → *tu comprar-<u>as</u>* 'you will buy'; *ellos*
<u>*han*</u> 'they have' → *ellos comprar-<u>an</u>* 'they will buy'; in McMahon
1994: 161). However, if the same process is extant in Language B, it
is virtually impossible to distinguish clearly whether the change in A
is occurring despite contact with B (and is therefore *natural*), or
because of it (and so is *non-natural*).

As can be seen, terminology such as *natural* and *non-natural* in being open to interpretation, typically results in ambiguity and *mis-interpretation*. This is exacerbated by the fact that such terms are also value-laden. As McMahon (1994: 267) points out, 'terms like "unnatural" in historical linguistics have often led to judgements of "undesirable" or the like ... and "natural" and "non-natural" are arguably just too close to "natural" and "unnatural" for comfort'. This has been a valid issue in the application of such labels to long-marginalized systems such as pidgins and creoles. Mühlhäusler (1986: 259–61) argues that to generally classify languages in such terms raises the question of equality between systems, which becomes particularly problematic with pidgins and creoles. For example, if we classify pidgins and creoles as favouring *non-natural* processes, then (given the associations that such a label carries) are we allowing them to be perceived as negligible systems (that is, unequal to *natural* languages)? Similarly, if they are instead catego-rized as systems where *natural* processes of change increasingly occur, does it therefore follow that they are 'equal' in every way to other languages which favour similar mechanisms, such as English? Most linguists would be uncomfortable with such generalized con-clusions and for many creolists, this would be a particularly sensitive issue, given the negative conceptions that have plagued pidgin and creole studies. Because of such concerns, it has been suggested that pidgins and creoles be defined without reference to such terminology. Pidgins, for example, could easily be categorized as systems which are less complex linguistically and more restricted in social function than 'full' languages such as English since they are used only for spe-cific purposes by people who already possess adequate native lan-guages. We could also add the specification that pidgins have the propensity to become 'full' creole languages if speakers require it.

It is, however, much more difficult to define creoles without rais-ing the notion of equality between systems (which is bound up in the natural/non-natural dichotomy). As stated in Section 1.2, they are fully fledged, linguistically adequate mother tongues that can be used in a range of different functions. Nevertheless, the social stigma that many of them have carried for at least some part of their lives has meant that they are not always recognized as such, even by native speakers, to many of whom they are 'broken' forms of different European languages. A lack of **codification** in many instances (discussed in Chapter 4) has significantly contributed to this: a creole is infrequently and inconsistently the medium of original or translated written material, which reinforces the perception that it is inadequate in this area. Thus native creole speakers often opt for a language (such as English in the Anglophone Caribbean) which will allow them the chance of social mobility; just as some native speakers of non-standard Englishes will cultivate competence in both written and spoken standard forms for use in situations that require it, such as reading academic textbooks and participating in certain job interviews.

Creoles may therefore be seen as socially unequal to other *natural* languages. Whinnom (1971: 109) stated that a creole speaker could in fact be said to be, in this sense, 'handicapped by his language'), but such a judgement is controversial and would doubtless engender 'emotionally loaded discussion' (1971: 109) among creolists and native speakers alike. Thus, the problems with potentially misleading nomenclature such as *natural/non-natural* (not to mention *equality*!) have come to be highlighted through their application to pidgins and creoles. As such, it has become increasingly apparent that such labels either have to be clearly re-defined or done away with completely (McMahon (1994: 267), for example, suggests instead the use of *internally motivated* and *externally motivated* changes).

1.3.3 Language acquisition and language learning

The question of how humans acquire language has been one of the more fascinating sub-disciplines of twentieth-century linguistics. While data from mono- and bi-lingual children and adults has proved invaluable in this area, it is possible that it can be productively supplemented by information from pidgins and creoles. For example, it has been postulated that since pidgins are used by adult speakers who already have individual native languages, they should exhibit features symptomatic of *second language learning* (an issue we will look at in more detail in Chapter 2). In fact, the processes that govern pidginization and second language learning (an example of which could be your learning a language such as French between the ages of 12 and 18) are very similar. In both, the learner is usually adolescent or adult, and the language being learned (known as L2) is either second or subsequent to her native language(s). The learning of the L2 is a conscious process, with the learner always cognizant of the target language, which may involve systematic teaching. The learner is also often aware of 'difficult' aspects of the L2's structure. Learning of the L2 may also cease before the learner is fluent, the outcome of which is often partial competence (adapted from Sebba 1997: 100). There have also been suggestions of possible parallels between creolization and *first language acquisition*.

The latter connection has been made in the wake of theories of genesis such as Bickerton's Language Bioprogram Hypothesis (explored in fuller detail in Chapter 2), which essentially states that many creoles are created by a pidgin-speaking community's first generation of children, whose genetic blueprint for shaping language is necessarily unleashed. Similarities between creolization (if Bickerton is right!) and first language acquisition include the fact that the person acquiring a native or first language (L1) is typically a child, for whom the enterprise is an unconscious process. The acquirer is unaware of the target and of its complexity, and there is no systematic teaching involved. It is also usual for the acquirer to become fluent and competent in the L1.

As yet, many of the links between pidginization, creolization, language learning and acquisition remain to be explored. However, this is an area where pidgin and creole data can contribute to a more thorough understanding of such processes, which may ultimately cast more light on how the human brain works.

These then, are some of the areas where work on pidgins and creoles has fed into linguistic enquiry. Now that we have defined Carrington's path and understood some more about the environs that it cuts through, we can start to examine some of its 'landmarks'. The next chapter really begins the story of pidgins and creoles by looking at theories of their genesis; Chapter 3 details the creole continuum, a model that attempts to encapsulate the variation found in many contemporary creole-using communities; and Chapter 4 closes this narrative with a discussion of language-planning policies that have been implemented in certain territories and which will therefore impact on the future of their creoles.

Endnotes

1. Creoles are generally named for the language that the majority of their vocabulary is taken from. Since this often tends to be the superstratal

language, it is the name of the latter which becomes enshrined in the label, which can take various forms, as in *Berbice Dutch*, *Berbice Dutch-based creole*, *Berbice Dutch-lexifier creole*.

2. Though this is a plausible scenario for the development of BD, it is noteworthy that the lack of information about the period means that, for the moment, it remains hypothetical (Holm 1989: 331).

3. The following historical account is adapted from Holm (1988: Chapter 2).

|2|

Once long ago, not too long ago
Theories of genesis

Creation is not an act but a process
> (Theodosius Dobzhansky, *Changing Man*)

[T]he more you look the more you see
> (Peter Grant, *Ecology and Evolution of Darwin's Finches*)

2.1 Introduction

In the last chapter, we looked at definitions and general types of pidgins and creoles. It should be becoming apparent that even though so many different types of pidgins and creoles exist all over the world, they share certain essential characteristics that justify their categorization as a distinct group. First, they are all formed in the context of a specific kind of language contact, where the situation is such that some kind of 'language bridge' has to be formed. Second, and perhaps as a consequence of this, many of the pidgins and creoles which have been studied indicate that this group (or at least certain members of the group) share particular linguistic features even though they are separated in time, geographical space and (as far as can be ascertained) have had no contact with each other. The question of why this should be, exactly why pidgins and creoles which have developed and are used independently of each other should share certain characteristics, has inevitably led scholars to investigate and theorize about their origins in the hope that 'the more we look' the more we may understand about the processes of linguistic creation.

This chapter will therefore look at various theories of genesis that have been proposed over the years. This has formed one of the central and more controversial debates in the field of creolistics, since such theories inevitably reflect a particular world view and in so doing, embody perspectives that are eventually challenged; something that should become clearer as we go on. I will follow Arends *et al.* (1995) in dividing theories of genesis into three groups (though there is sometimes overlap between them). The first consists of theories that take the superstratal language as their starting point; the second includes a hypothesis which emphasizes the importance of substratal languages; and the third, one that is based on universals of language acquisition.

2.2 The superstratal target

As stated in Chapter 1 (Section 1.3.1), when creole usage first came to notice in the seventeenth century, it was in the context of European colonial and commercial expansion overseas. The first records of pidgins and creoles and of their usage were therefore made by European traders, merchants, navigators and travellers, whose 'world' was based on the idea of European dominance and superiority in all things. The first assumptions about the genesis of these languages were inevitably, therefore, heavily Eurocentric. This is evident in the earliest writings about pidgins and creoles, where comparisons with European languages (which naturally functioned as a point of reference) were frequent and often unfavourable; typifying these languages as deviant or 'bastardizations'. As such, early ideas about pidgin and creole origins were often based on assumptions of deviance from a European ideal, and certain formal genesis theories were constructed against this background, even though they took shape much later. We shall now look at some of the most well known in a bit more detail.

2.2.1 *Foreigner Talk theory*

If you have ever been in a situation where you have had to use your native language to someone who does not speak it fluently, you will already have an inkling of what is entailed in the Foreigner Talk theory of genesis. If, for example, you have ever been asked by a non-native speaker of your language for directions to a certain place, you may have noticed that you automatically modified your language use in an attempt to make yourself understandable. The strategies you employed were very likely those of *simplification* (which appear to be universal to speakers of any language) and the result would have been what is commonly known as Foreigner Talk (FT). Arends *et al.* (1995: 95–8) state that FT is the result of separate processes such as *accommodation, imitation* and *telegraphic condensation*. As the following example illustrates, Speaker A, a native English speaker, *accommodates* to the fact that B is a non-native speaker. This 'results in slower speech, shorter and less complex sentences, the introduction of pauses between constitutents, the use of general and semantically unspecific terms, and repetitions' (Arends *et al.* 1995: 95), as in:

1 A: Could you please repeat the problem that your wife was mentioning?
    B: What you say?
    A: Your wife has a problem, a difficulty … Please say it again, please repeat the problem … Please say it again.

In order to facilitate comprehension, A will sometimes *imitate* the structures that B produces, thus 'reinforcing' them:

2 A: I no hear vot you say.
    B: You no hear?

A may also delete lexical items known as *function words* from her speech. These are words such as articles, auxiliary verbs and copulas ('linking' verbs such as *to be*) which primarily serve a grammatical function in utterances. This is known as *telegraphic condensation*, since it results in the condensed language typical of telegrams:

3 A: Did you get the package that was sent from Hong Kong?
    B: What you say?
    A: Package arrive Hong Kong. You get?

(All examples from Arends et al. 1995: 95–7)

It has been hypothesized that since all of these processes seem to be universally employed in situations where one speaker has to make herself understood to another/others who are not fluent in her native language; planters on New World plantations, for example, would also have made use of them in initial communication with their slaves.[1] The germ of this idea has been attributed to Schuchardt, writing in the nineteenth century:

> For the master and the slave it was simply a matter of mutual comprehension. The master stripped off from the European

language everything that was peculiar to it, the slave surpressed everything in it that was distinctive. They met on a middle ground ... [but] to a lesser extent at the very beginning. The white man was the teacher of the black man. At first the black man mimicked him.

(Quoted in Holm 1988: 33–4)

As an illustration of his theory, Schuchardt highlighted cases such as that of Lingua Franca (spoken in the Mediterranean area), where verbs often have a form derived from the Romance infinitive. FT theory predicts that the Romance speaker in the initial contact situation would, in an attempt at simplification, use the 'base' or unconjugated form of the verb which is, of course, the infinitive.

Later explicit proponents of FT theory asserted that characteristic features of pidgins, such as simple structures, the use of repetition and of a limited, general vocabulary, were also the result of the processes of FT. Naro (1978) for example, hypothesized that West African Pidgin Portuguese (WAPP: see Chapter 1, Section 1.3.2) emerged not in Africa but in Portugal as a reconaissance language, or a form of Portuguese simplified by FT processes that was taught to African interpreters. However, Arends *et al.* (1995: 95) point out that there is a danger of circularity to such arguments. Models of FT have been based on perceived similarities with pidgins, so 'the latter may erroneously be thought to have emerged out of the former' (Arends *et al.* 1995: 97). In addition, it would seem that FT theory does not adequately cover all cases of genesis. For example, FT in Dutch, especially that directed at low-status foreigners,[2] is typically OV (Object Verb) in structure:

Tafels   schoonmaken!

tables   clean!   = 'clean [the] tables!'

FT theory would therefore predict that this OV structure would have been passed into the pidgins (and ultimately creoles) that resulted from the colonial language contact between Dutch planters and African slaves. However, Dutch-lexifier creoles such as Negerhollands and Berbice Dutch have SVO (Subject Verb Object) structures. It could be surmised that the slaves' native language(s) may have favoured SVO order but it is known that the main substratal parent for Berbice Dutch Creole, Eastern Ijo, is an SOV language. Interestingly, the high production of SVO patterns is characteristic of second-language (L2) learners of Dutch (Arends *et al.* 1995: 97). This brings us to our second theory of genesis: the Imperfect L2 Learning Hypothesis.

2.2.2 *The Imperfect L2 Learning Hypothesis*

As we have seen, the FT theory of genesis assumes a cyclic process of simplification and mimicry: native speaker A, in accommodating to B's non-native speaker competence, simplifies her own language through various processes. B mimics these simplifications to A, A mimics them back and the structures are so reinforced and passed into a resultant pidgin, and ultimately, extended pidgin or creole. The Imperfect L2 Learning Hypothesis, however, assumes no accommodation of A to B. According to this theory, A will make little or no concession to the fact that B does not speak her language fluently (if at all). B therefore has to try to 'keep up' with A's native competence and, inevitably, will make certain 'mistakes' which are universal to all second-language learners. If the relationship between A and B incorporates something of a teacher–student role, A will 'correct' B, helping the latter to acquire the rules of that particular language and so achieve fluency. However, if A is a planter and B a slave, the relationship is such that the latter's 'mistakes' will go unchecked and will eventually become part of the resultant pidgin (and creole) structure.

The idea that L2 learning played a part in pidgin and creole genesis was first put forward by Coelho, a nineteenth-century Portuguese philologist:

> The Romance and creole dialects, Indo-Portuguese and all the similar formations represent the first stage or stages in the acquisition of a foreign language by a people that speaks or spoke another. ... They owe their origin to the operation of psychological laws that are everywhere the same and not to the influence of the former languages among whom these dialects are found.
>
> (Coelho 1880: 193, 195; quoted in Holm 1988: 27)

His proposal has since been lent weight by research into L2 processes, which has isolated certain features that are also found in many pidgins and creoles. These include:

- invariant verb forms, possibly derived from the infinitive, as in

he see she and ask she to go t'eatre
'he saw her and asked her to go to the cinema'

- invariable placement of the negator before the main verb, as in *me na know wha' you talkin' 'bout*
'I don't know what you're talking about'.

Arends *et al.* (1995: 129) cite examples of this process in the usage of second language learners of English and German, who produce utterances such as *he no eat* (vs standard English *he doesn't/didn't eat*) and *Ich nix arbeite* (vs standard German *Ich arbeite nicht* 'I don't/didn't work').

- Fixed single word order, so that there is often no inversion in questions:
you have cigarette? (the question is indicated instead by rising intonation)
'Have you/ do you have any cigarettes?'

- Reduced or absent plural marking:
she see four box inside
'she saw four boxes inside'.

There are of course other features of pidgins and creoles that cannot be accounted for by this theory, but it is highly probable that it played some role in their formation.

Both FT and Imperfect L2 Learning theories, in highlighting the mechanisms of acquiring the superstratal target, overlap with universalist thought in subscribing to the idea of *polygenesis,* 'many beginnings', first voiced in the nineteenth century and whose base assumption is that 'the human mind is the same in every clime, and accordingly we find nearly the same process adopted in the formation of language in every country' (Greenfield 1830: 48; quoted in Holm 1988: 22). Todd reinforced this in 1974:

> there are universal patterns of linguistic behaviour appropriate to contact situations ... pidgins and creoles are alike because fundamentally, languages are alike and simplification processes are alike ... human beings are biologically programmed to acquire *Language.*

> (Todd 1974: 42)

Thus, the cognitive processes which operate in certain situations of contact are worthy of investigation in formulating ideas on pidgin and creole genesis. We shall return to this in Section 2.4.

2.2.3 *Nautical jargon theory*

It has long been noted that many English- and French-lexifier creoles contain a nautical element in their vocabulary. Speakers of Krio (an English-lexifier creole spoken in Sierra Leone, West Africa), for example, make use of the following items ('j' denotes the sound [j], as in *year*):

gjali (galley), meaning 'kitchen'
kjapsaj (capsize), meaning 'overturn'
bambotgjal (bumboat girl), meaning 'prostitute'.

Sranan, an English-lexifier creole spoken in Suriname, also has this element, present in words such as *drifi* (drift = 'draw up'), and *ari* (haul = 'pull/draw'). French-lexifier creoles from Louisiana to the Indian Ocean also contain words with a nautical ancestry, such as *hale/rale* (haler = 'pull/drag'), *mare* (amarrer = 'tie') and *hele/rele* (heler = 'call') (Arends *et al.* 1995: 92).

One explanation for the widespread presence of such terms has been that English and French sailors, including those on slave ships, created and made use of a nautical jargon which was eventually passed on to individual substratal groups (for example, slaves in the Caribbean and America; indentured labourers in the Pacific). The latter, in using the jargon as a main means of communication, eventually turned it into a stable pidgin and, ultimately, an extended pidgin or creole. Robertson (1971: 13–14; cited in Mühlhäusler 1986: 97) subscribes to this theory in his outline of the formation of Melanesian Pidgin English (of which New Guinea Pidgin English (see Chapter 1, Section 1.2) is a variety):

Take one sea full of British sailormen, hard, daring, very British and profane, and leave it in a cool place for two days; extract their speech; then bring to the boil and extract what speech remains. Add a coconut shell each of Chinese, Malay, German and Kanaka and bring to the boil a hundred or so times, then season with a little war or two; add a few drops of Mission sauce and sprinkle with blackbirder pepper and recruiter salt. Strain through Kanaka [Polynesian 'Pacific Islander'] lips and serve with beer, or with undiluted Australian any other time.

Robertson's basic assumption of the significance of sailors in the formation of such languages had earlier (and more seriously) been expressed by Reinecke (1937), who stated that 'the seaman is a figure of the greatest importance in the creation of the more permanent makeshift tongues'. Faine (1939; cited in Mühlhäusler 1986), in this vein, theorized that a 'maritime French', once used on French slave ships and those that traded in American ports, had evolved into French-lexifier creoles in the New World. Hall (1966: 120) had also postulated the existence of a seventeenth-century proto-nautical English, which would have been in use 'somewhere in the lower reaches of the Thames, on either bank of the river, in the docks of London ... and in other English seaports such as Plymouth'.

Nautical jargon theory has, however, come to play a fairly marginal role in the genesis debates for various reasons. First, and very importantly, it is difficult to define exactly what any proto-nautical jargon may have been like. Churchill for example, who stated that sailors had been integral to the formation of South Seas Beach-la-Mar, or Bislama (the variety of Melanesian Pidgin English spoken in Vanautu), only cites anecdotal evidence for the existence of an influential nautical English (Churchill 1911; cited in Mühlhäusler 1986: 98). Hall's (1966) description of seventeenth-century nautical English is also problematic, since it is unlikely that it existed as a uniform entity, varying instead (as jargons do, see Chapter 1) from ship to ship, even sailor to sailor. In addition, there would seem to have been a great deal of overlap between features of this purported jargon and of varieties of non-standard English, which could just as easily have been passed on by plantation owners and overseers in British colonies. Baker (1982: 243; quoted in Mühlhäusler 1986: 99), in discussing Faine's theory, also points out that 'there is nothing to indicate that just one 'nautical patois' existed, or that the collective expertise of sailors in communicating with non-Francophones would have equipped them all with a single uniform [maritime French]'.

Second, there is no satisfactory explanation as to how sailors would have transmitted their jargon(s) to substratal groups, since 'precise learning contexts, the time of exposure and other social variables remain unknown' (Mühlhäusler 1986: 98). This is, of course, a perennial problem in creole studies generally, so such a criticism may seem unduly harsh. However, what we do know about particular contact environments makes certain scenarios implausible. Take, for example, the postulated transfer of a jargon from sailors to slaves. Historical sources state that slaves spent the majority of their time on ships chained below decks, with a minimum of contact with their keepers. Slave ships were miserable, potentially dangerous places: the presence of a large number of frightened, ill-treated human beings makes for a volatile situation. Crews therefore limited their interaction with their cargo: sailors, for example, would only go into the hold when the slaves had been taken on deck for exercise, or if force-feeding certain 'miscreants' was considered necessary. On the whole, it would seem that there would have been little opportunity and, importantly, little motivation for the sailors to have transmitted anything linguistically substantial, and potentially unifying (again, a dangerous prospect) to their captives.

Finally, there is the simple fact that the presence of nautical items (such as those cited on page 43) in an extended pidgin or creole's lexicon is not unequivocal evidence of a proto-nautical jargon, though it has been taken as such by supporters of this theory. The fact that many pidgins and creoles began to evolve at a time when the ship, and hence the port, was the only means of contact with the outside world may account for their eventual incorporation of culture-specific items such as *bumbotgjal* to label prostitutes that frequented the docks. In addition, the majority of the world's pidgins and creoles exist in coastal and island territories (see the maps at the front of this book), thus making terms such as *kjapsaj* 'overturn' and *drifi* 'drift' not necessarily the residue of a sailor's jargon but, instead, the inevitable usage of people who live near the sea. The role of the sailors in pidgin and creole genesis, therefore, 'remains to be proven' (Mühlhäusler 1986: 99).

Even though each of the theories in this section approaches the question of pidgin and creole genesis in a different way, we would be justified in saying that they all essentially stress the importance of the superstratal language. Nautical jargon theory, for example, is based purely on elements that have been derived from different superstratal languages. FT theory assumes that the native superstratal speaker starts off and reinforces the mechanism of simplification for the substratal speaker, for whom the superstratal language is a target. The Imperfect L2 Learning theory also assumes that the substratal speaker has the acquisition of the superstratal language as her target. Thus, the underlying assumption of both theories is that in the pidgin and creole formation environment, 'the same mental factor was at work, namely the imperfect mastery of a [superstratal] language' (Jespersen 1922: 233–4). In the following section, we shall look at a theory that shifts the locus of pidgin and creole formation from Europe to Africa: that of *monogenesis*.

2.3 The substratal essence

2.3.1 *Monogenesis*

Hellinger (1985: 45) has suggested that in the 1930s the center of gravity of creole studies shifted from the Old World to the New.

(Holm 1988: 36)

Hellinger's statement not only refers to the fact that native creole speakers began, in the early twentieth century, to research and write about their languages; but also implies that this was accompanied by a general change in perspective. In the vanguard of this shift was the work of the Herskovitses, a husband and wife anthropological team who had worked in West Africa before moving on to study Caribbean cultures and languages. Their conclusion on the make-up of the creoles they encountered 'from the Sea Islands of South Carolina to Suriname in South America', was that 'Negroes [*sic*] have been using words from European languages to render literally the underlying morphological patterns of West African tongues' (Herskovits 1936: 131; in Holm 1988: 37). This statement was to catalyse a new approach to the pidgin/creole genesis question; namely, looking at the importance of substratal languages.

A precedent for such work had been set in the nineteenth century with Lucien Adams who, in comparing features of Atlantic French-lexifier creoles and various West African languages, had proposed the idea that a creole's grammatical and phonological system was inherited from the substrata and the lexicon from the the superstratum:

> the Guinea Negroes, transported to those [Caribbean] colonies, took words from French but retained as far as possible the phonology and grammar of their mother tongues. ... The grammar is no other than the general grammar of the languages of Guinea

(1883: 47; quoted in Holm 1988: 28)

The Herskovitses' study gave impetus to this approach to creole research: one where pidgins and creoles, and by extension the cultures for which they were vehicles, were not 'corruptions' or 'deviations' of European forms, but instead incorporated features retained from an African ancestry. Thus in 1927, for example, Lichtveld described Sranan as having 'almost all the outer and inner character-istics of an African language' (quoted in Holm 1988: 37) and as we saw in Chapter 1 (Section 1.3.2), Suzanne Sylvain's 1936 doctoral thesis stated that Haitian French-lexifier creole was an Ewe language with a French vocabulary.

It was the 1950s, however, that saw a coherent theory of substratal influence in pidgin/creole genesis emerge. In 1956, Whinnom sug-gested that a Portuguese-lexifier creole from Ternate which had been transported to the Philippines in the seventeenth century had grown into the latter's Spanish-lexifier creole. Taylor (1959) pointed out that many of the Portuguese features in the Philippine Spanish-lexi-fier creole were also in many Caribbean creoles. On the basis of these findings, a paper delivered by Thompson at the first conference on pidgin and creole studies (held at the Mona, Jamaica campus of the University of the West Indies, 1959) postulated the existence of a Portuguese extended proto-pidgin from which many creoles, particu-larly those of the Atlantic region, had sprung; and the theory of *monogenesis*, 'one beginning', was born. This West African Pidgin Portuguese (WAPP) was supposedly spoken between the fifteenth and eighteenth centuries in and around the numerous forts and trading settlements that had been established by those pioneers of the slave trade, the Portuguese, on the West African coast (Holm 1988). The suggested structure of WAPP was along the lines proposed by the Herskovitses, Lichtveld and Sylvain: its grammar and phonology was derived from the substrata, and its lexicon from superstratal Portuguese (see Chapter 1, Section 1.3.2). Slaves awaiting trans-portation to the New World on the West African coast learnt WAPP and subsequently took it to the new environments in which they found themselves. However, New World colonies were run not only by the Portuguese but also by other European powers. These ex-colonies are now home to English-, Dutch- and French-lexifier cre-oles, for example. How, then, could these derive from WAPP? Taylor (1959) hypothesized that WAPP speakers changed their vocabulary in the individual New World environments that became their homes. Thus if WAPP-speaking slaves ended up in a colony where English was the superstratal language, they exchanged their Portuguese vocabulary for an English one; a process Stewart (1962: 42) termed *relexification*. The grammatical structure of WAPP was, however, retained, which would account for the grammatical and structural similarities found among creoles with different superstratal parents and which appear to have had no contact with each other.

The concepts of monogenesis and relexification held sway during the 60s and early 70s but are now no longer widely supported as a generic theory of creole genesis, largely because it really has only ever referred to the creoles of the Caribbean Atlantic region. However, neither has been wholly discredited: Sebba (1997: 74), for example, outlines a case of relexification in Media Lengua, a *mixed language* (see Chapter 1, Section 1.3.2) spoken in Ecuador; and monogenesis has generated offshoot theories, such as the Domestic Hypothesis.

The latter was first put forward by Hancock in 1986, and was restricted to tracing the origins of the English-lexifier creoles of the Atlantic Caribbean region. Hancock proposed that this group had indeed emerged from 'one beginning'; not through a process of relexification from WAPP, but instead from a 'Guinea Coast Creole English' (GCCE; in itself a development of an earlier English-lexifier proto-pidgin) used on the West African coast in the seventeenth century. This creole was purportedly transmitted to slaves awaiting tranportation on the West African coast, and so eventually taken to the New World. Once there, these slaves found themselves in very different contact situations:

> in Suriname, speakers familiar with Guinea Coast Creole English ... were outnumbered by those who spoke only African languages and outnumbered in turn speakers of regional British dialects. In parts of the Caribbean the same components came together, except that those arriving with a knowledge of [Guinea Coast] Creole were outnumbered by speakers of metropolitan English, as in Barbados, or Saba, or the Caymans.
>
> (Hancock 1986: 95)

This interaction between GCCE, dialectal English and monolingual African language speakers, 'in different proportions in different places' (Hancock 1986) essentially gave rise to individual daughter creoles. Thus, the linguistic similarities shared by the latter are due to their common progenitor, GCCE; and their differences, to the diversity of the 'componential matrix', or the components of the speech community, in each environment.

The Domestic Hypothesis offers an intriguing possibility for the genesis of the Caribbean English-lexifier creoles, but there are problems with some of Hancock's assumptions. For example, he states that one of the reasons why a mother creole like GCCE is likely to have existed is that the Caribbean English-lexifier creoles 'form a genetically and historically related group'. This may be true, but does not necessarily testify to a common ancestor on the West African coast. There is instead a very real possibility that these creoles are 'related' because they developed in similar environments in similar circumstances, with dialectal forms of one superstratal language, English, in the New World. The similarities between these creoles may have been further added to by migration of English-lexifier creole speakers throughout British-held Caribbean territories. Caribbean plantation societies often consisted of mobile populations, with planters and slaves frequently moving to larger, richer, more fertile islands (cf. Chapter 1, Section 1.3.1 on social instability). Trinidad, for example, was inundated with planters and their slaves from French-held islands in 1777, when the Spanish opened it to Catholic migration; and again in 1797 (when it was surrendered to Britain) by migrants from the British Caribbean. Thus today, Trinidad's French-lexifier creole shares similarities with those of Martinique and Guadeloupe, and its English-lexifier creole with that of Barbados. The Domestic Hypothesis, however, makes no mention of the importance of such factors in accounting for similarities between creoles.

The social context that Hancock envisaged as giving rise to GCCE is also problematic. He assumed that it emerged from a particular domestic set-up (hence the name of the theory): British White males, involved in the slave trade, settled on the West African coast, married local African women and had Creole (here meaning 'mixed-race') offspring. These British also worked in close proximity to other local Africans. According to Hancock, five distinct social groups emerged in this community: (1) the resident Whites, (2) their Creole offspring, (3) the *grumettoes* or Africans who worked for the Europeans and eventually for the Creoles, (4) the indigenous population and (5) the slaves awaiting shipment. The first two groups had 'knowledge of the emerging creole' but 'it was native only to the Afro-Europeans [Creoles], the population of which was steadily increasing and which came to outnumber that of their White fathers by the end of the 1600s' (Hancock 1986: 81).

Thus, Hancock assumes that GCCE would have emerged out of the 'marriages' of British men and African women, who would supposedly have used a proto-pidgin (see page 48) to communicate. Children born to these unions would then have aided in turning it into a creole, GCCE, in acquiring it as a native tongue. Though a plausible scenario for the development of a creole, certain social factors suggest that it may not have been possible.

For example, British settlers were a minority among the indigenous population: in 1620, there was a settlement of eight British subjects on the coast, and in 1721, thirty on Bunce Island, Sierra Leone (Hancock 1986). It is therefore highly possible that instead of developing a pidgin for use with the Africans, they assimilated to the cultural and linguistic mores of the larger group. Alternatively, if the men were temporary settlers (and Hancock points out that many were), they may have learnt enough of the dominant African language to get by, and/or taught their workers a rudimentary form of English; but on the whole, may have treated their African 'wives' as transient liasons, and any offspring as the mother's responsibility. In fact, Hancock indicates that this may indeed have been the case. He quotes Snelgrave (1734: 256–7), who provides some insight into the nature of European-African marriages: 'some White men that lived there did not scruple to lend their Black Wives to the Pirates, purely on account of the great Rewards they gave'. He also quotes Matthews (1985: 170–1), who ironically casts doubt on the existence of a creole as a native language of the Afro-European offspring: 'several White men, natives of Great Britain, are now resident in the country [Africa], who have remained there upwards to twenty years; *but their African born children speak no other language than their mothers*' (emphasis mine). He goes on to state that even Creoles who were sent to England to learn 'White man's book, on their return to their native country immediately reassume the manner of living and embrace the superstitious customs and ceremonies of their countrymen' (Matthews 1985; quoted in Hancock 1986: 82). Thus, it would seem that Creole or Afro-European offspring generally learnt the languages of their mothers as native tongues and that others, whose British fathers took an interest in them, may have been bilingual in English as well. However, the cultures of the African mothers would appear to have predominated in the social shaping of these children, since even those who had been sent to England obviously felt more comfortable in their maternal heritage. It would therefore seem that the African women were mainly little more than concubines, and that they were sole carers for their Creole children; a situation that must have been even more pointed when the White fathers did not settle permanently.

A further point of concern in the Domestic Hypothesis is the transmission of GCCE (if it did in fact exist) to slaves. Hancock's assumption is that the grumettoes learnt GCCE from the Creoles with whom they eventually intermarried, and used it amongst themselves. Since the duties of the grumettoes included first capturing and then guarding slaves as they awaited shipment, they were principally responsible for transmitting GCCE to the latter during the time they were held on the coast. There are several problems with this hypothesis. First, Hancock himself states that the grumettoes 'were local Africans who lived near, and worked for, the Europeans and the Creoles, *while maintaining their own ethnic identity*' (1986: 82–3; emphasis mine): a task that would not have been especially difficult since the majority were people of the Sherbo, especially Kru, tribe. They were therefore unlikely to use GCCE when they were working together. Traders were also very aware of the dangers that could arise from a group of captive slaves who could communicate easily with each other: 'cautions where a cargo is of one language is so much more the requisite' (Atkins 1721: 172; in Hancock 1986) and therefore, 'while it was not always possible, efforts were made to keep slaves speaking the same language separate from each other' (Hancock 1986: 84). Why, then, would grumettoes be given the time and opportunity to teach GCCE to the slaves? Indeed, traders tried to ensure that no single group of slaves was held for long periods on the coast, out of safety and financial considerations. The likelihood of high mortality rates among scared and frequently weakened captives, plus inadequate holding resources for a continuous turnover of slaves meant that long periods of imprisonment on the coast increased the possibility of low financial returns. Thus, the transmission of a creole during this period would have been thwarted by time and safety factors. An additional point is that New World planters tried to keep speakers of any one African language to a minimum on their plantations (cf. Chapter 1, Section 1.2). If the slaves had in fact gone to their new lives speaking a common creole, it is very strange indeed that measures were instigated there to separate them on the basis of their native languages.

The final issue concerns the transformation of GCCE in the New World into different English-lexifier creoles. As stated on page 48, Hancock accounts for this through the differences in the linguistic composition of the population in individual environments. This, however, is a difficult claim to substantiate and given that the process is reduced simply to the interaction of 'different proportions [of speakers] in different places', seems to have 'been reached on the bases of assumption rather than from any detailed examination of the languages in question and their individual histories', a criticism that Hancock (1986: 71) himself makes of other genesis accounts. In summary, though the Domestic Hypothesis provides an interesting explanation for the genesis of a certain group of creoles, there is 'in fact little in the way of direct evidence' (Arends *et al.* 1995: 91) that, at the moment, could help validate it.

2.4 The universalist dimension

The theories we have looked at thus far have, on the whole, tended to stress the importance of either the superstratal or substratal parent in genesis. While the contribution of both parent language groups is undeniably important, we cannot help (as stated earlier) but consider the very real possibility that the cognitive processes that 'kick in' in certain situations of language contact may also have played a significant role. The following section therefore sets out one of the most well-known and controversial theories of creole genesis in the field: the Language Bioprogram Hypothesis.

2.4.1 *The Language Bioprogram Hypothesis*

As we have seen, one of the things that many theories of genesis assume is that creoles are born out of an earlier form (usually a pidgin) which stabilizes. However, Bickerton in 1981 questioned this assumption: what if there was no such integral link between a pidgin and creole? What if the development of a creole has more to do with the innate devices of first language (L1) acquisition than with a gradual evolution from a pidgin, which may be the result of adult L2 learning (see Chapter 1, Section 1.3.3)?

The Language Bioprogram Hypothesis (LBH) was not formulated to account for the genesis of all creoles; Bickerton (1981: 3) explicitly stated that his primary interest lay 'in situations where the normal continuity of language transmission is most severely disrupted'. Though creoles generally result from processes of abnormal transmission (see Chapter 1, Section 1.3.2), not all are formed in situations where there is a 'catastrophic break in linguistic tradition that is unparalleled' (Sankoff 1979: 24; quoted in Bickerton 1981). For example, the French-lexifier creole of Réunion developed in close contact with its superstratal language and so resembles it to a very high degree. Tok Pisin, the lingua franca of Papua New Guinea, evolved in co-existence with the indigenous (and substratal) languages of the majority of its speakers, and so incorporates many features from the latter. However, in what Bickerton calls the 'classic creole situation', the emergent creole-speaking community mainly comprises people who have 'been torn' from their native cultures; whose native languages (the substrata) are evaluated unfavourably and, also, who have limited access to a superimposed (superstratal) language. 'Classic' creoles also have two main defining properties. First, they are languages which emerged in situations where a pidgin had been in use for a very short period: no more than one generation. Second, the composition of the population in such creole-formation environments was clearly stratified: no more than 20 per cent were superstratal speakers, and the remaining 80 per cent were linguistically diverse. Consequently, creoles which arise out of such situations share a particular set of features, despite the fact that they developed in geographic isolation from each other and with different substratal and superstratal parents. One could perhaps assert that this is due to the workings of monogenesis: a hypothetical proto-pidgin carried to different areas split into different pidgins, nevertheless retaining certain proto-pidgin structures, which were eventually inherited by resultant creoles. However, Bickerton (1981) stated that in his test case, that of Hawaiian Pidgin English (HPE) and Hawaiian Creole English (HCE), the distinctive 'classic' creole features of the latter were not in the former. In other words, it would seem that HCE did not develop gradually out of HPE. If this is the case, and if such discontinuity of transmission is apparent for other 'classic' creoles, the question of where similarities across classic creoles come from requires an answer other than monogenesis.

Between 1973 and 1974, Bickerton and his team had carried out extensive fieldwork in Hawaii, recording data from speakers of HPE and HCE. For approximately a century after Europe's colonization of this area, the population had remained primarily comprised of indigenous Hawaiians (speaking their native language) but also incorporated a small but increasing minority of native English speakers. Nevertheless, the language of the sugar plantations, worked as they were by native Hawaiians, was Hawaiian. However, in 1876, the sugar industry began to increase its output (because of a revision of US tariff laws to allow the free importation of Hawaiian sugar), causing a huge influx of workers from areas such as China, Portugal, Japan, Korea, the Philippines and Puerto Rico. Out of this multilingual community emerged, sometime between 1900 and 1920, HPE.

Bickerton's HPE speakers, aged 70–90, had arrived in Hawaii sometime between 1907 and 1930, already fluent in their individual native languages. He found that their HPE, in addition to being

extremely rudimentary and having little syntactic consistency, also
displayed high levels of interference from each speaker's native language which could, for example, differentiate a Japanese HPE
speaker from one of Filipino ancestry. Thus, 'anyone (in particular a
child) trying to learn HPE would have encountered formidable obstacles to even figuring out what the rules of HPE were supposed to be'
(Bickerton 1981: 13). Yet HCE speakers who were exposed to this
elementary, unstable HPE as children acquired complex, rule-governed features that are now part of the creole. In addition, 'the era-
sure of group differences in that [later] generation was complete. Even
other locally born persons cannot determine the ethnic background
of an HCE speaker by his speech alone, although the same person can
readily identify that of an HPE speaker by listening to him for a few
seconds' (Bickerton 1981: 15). Clearly, then, something extraordinary had occurred in the production of HCE; there appear to have
been 'extremely abrupt changes which took place while the first creole generation was growing to maturity' (Bickerton 1981: 17).

Since 'classic creoles' emerge very rapidly, within 20–30 years of
initial settlement, there had been no time for a 'stable, systematic, referentially adequate pidgin' to evolve among the adults of that community who, because of their age, appeared to be unable to concoct
anything other than an elementary form of communication. Thus, in
areas that produced such creoles (such as Hawaii and many of the
Caribbean plantation islands), there may have been a 'a highly variable, extremely rudimentary language' or jargon in existence (see
Chapter 1, Section 1.2) which would have had to serve as the 'language input' for a new generation. The children of this new generation would have been in an exceptional linguistic situation, since the
typical child is born into a family and community with a 'ready-
made, custom-validated, referentially adequate' (Bickerton 1981: 5)
language. Thus, carers are normally fluent native speakers of a language that has been around for a very long time and which therefore
has an established system of rules and patterns of discourse. Such
children therefore acquire and become fluent in their native language
through the help of their carers. However, the children in Bickerton's
scenario could not have had such assistance:

> [they] have, instead, something which may be quite adequate for
> emergency use, but which is quite unfit to serve as anyone's pri-
> mary tongue; which by reason of its variability, does not present
> even the little it offers in a form that would permit anyone to

learn it; and which the parent, with the best will in the world, cannot teach, since that parent knows no more of the language than the child (and will pretty soon know less). Everywhere else in the world it goes without saying that the parent knows more language than the child; here, if the child is to have an adequate language, he must speedily outstrip the knowledge of the parent.

(Bickerton 1981: 5)

The linguistic disadvantage postulated for these children would have been countered, in Bickerton's view, by their 'biological need' for a native tongue. They therefore turned the insufficient linguistic input they received into a fully fledged language (a creole) by 'running it through' an innate system universal to us all: the language bioprogram.

Theoretically, the bioprogram is a 'neurally encoded, genetically transmitted set of instructions' (McMahon 1994: 272) that specifies certain semantic and syntactic features. Bickerton asserts that these features were the first to appear in linguistic evolution, and that they still recur in the early speech of *any* child acquiring *any* language, be it English, Welsh, Russian or Saramaccan. This is 'biological language'; a 'genetic program for language which is [a child's] hominid inheritance' and which 'unrolls exactly as does the genetic program that determines his increase in size, muscular control, etc.' (Bickerton 1981: 296). However, over thousands of years, language has also developed a culture-specific aspect: different languages have come to encode features that diverge from a biological base, but which have emerged from cultural evolution. Thus, in 'normal' cases of language acquisition, the child's biological language will specify, for example, the lack of inversion in questions (a feature of child English and child German), but exposure to cultural language will throw up instances of inversion, which she will very likely come to adopt as a fluent native English or German speaker. However, for the child born into a situation where the availability of 'cultural language hit a bad patch' (Bickerton 1981: 296), 'biological language' is the only resort: the bioprogram kicks in, stirs the primeval soup of the unstable jargon, and language evolution begins once again. Thus, features like non-inversion of questions, a 'biological structure', remain encoded in many classic creoles, as do others such as the use of adjectives as verbs (*a gon full Angela bucket* 'I'm going to fill Angela's bucket'), also a feature of child English. As Bickerton (1981: 185) states, many so-called errors in child language 'would have been grammatical if the child had been learning a creole language'.

In 1984, Bickerton relaxed his original criteria for defining 'classic' creole status and conceded that languages which had evolved out of stable pidgins could also be included. The result was that creoles could be categorized in terms of distance from the bioprogram. This would depend on linguistic and demographic considerations: essentially, the more 'catastrophic' the circumstances in the creole-formation environment, the more bioprogram features the emergent creole would display. However, creoles developed in situations where there is a stable pidgin and/or access to superstratal or substratal languages (as in the case of Réunion Creole and Tok Pisin) would draw on these 'cultural language' models, and so be farther away from the bioprogram.

But what exactly are these bioprogram features? Bickerton (1981) isolates 12 syntactic and semantic features characteristic of 'classic creoles' but which, on the basis of comparisons between HCE and HPE, are unlikely to have appeared in their antecedent systems. Such creoles show evidence of the following characteristics:

1 *Movement rules* which allow speakers to move constituents into sentence-initial position for emphasis (as in HCE *o, daet wan ai si* 'Oh, that one I saw' = 'Oh, I saw that one') (Bickerton 1986: 19).
2 An *article system* whereby:
   (i) a definite article is used for all noun phrases (NPs) that have a specific reference and which can be assumed to be known to the listener, as in HCE *aefta da* [definite article] *boi, da wan wen jink daet milk, awl da mout soa* 'afterward, the mouth of the boy who had drunk that milk was all sore' (Bickerton 1986: 23);
   (ii) an indefinite article is used for all NPs that have a specific reference but which can be assumed to be unknown to the listener, as in HCE *hi get wan* [indefinite article] *blaek buk* 'he has a black book' (Bickerton 1986: 23);
   (iii) no (zero) article is used for a non-specific NP, as in HCE *(Ø) hu go daun frs iz (Ø) luza* 'the one who goes down first is the loser' (Bickerton 1986: 24).
3 A system whereby *tense, modality* and *aspect* are expressed by three individual morphemes that occur before the main verb (that is, in preverbal position). When two or more of these markers are used, they always occur in that order (that is, the *tense* marker always occurs before the *modal* or *aspectual* marker; the *modal*

marker always before the *aspectual*). The *tense* morpheme, such as *bin* in HCE, marks the grammatical category known as [+ anterior], which expresses 'past before past' in active verbs and 'past' in stative verbs. The *modality* morpheme (*go/gon* in HCE) marks [+ irrealis], which includes the expression of 'futures' and 'conditionals'; and the *aspectual* (HCE *stei*), the category of [+ nonpunctual] which denotes the 'progressive' and the 'habitual' forms of the verb. An example of *tense* and *tense + modal* marking can be seen in the following Guyanese English-lexifier creole (GC) utterance:

if   mi   <u>bin sii</u>   am,   mi   <u>bin go tel</u>   am
If   I   <u>had seen</u> him, I   <u>would have told</u> him
(Bickerton 1986: 24)

bin (tense [+anterior]) + *sii* (main active verb) = 'past before past' action
bin (tense [+ anterior]) + *go* (*mood* [+ irrealis]) + *tel* (main active verb) = past conditional action (because the telling was conditional on the speaker seeing someone).

4 A system whereby *verbal complements* stating realized and unrealized events are indicated by different means, as in:
HCE
   (i)   *ai gata <u>go</u> haia wan kapinta <u>go</u> fiks da fom* 'I had <u>to</u> hire a carpenter <u>to</u> fix the form' (realised event: complement introduced by *go*)
   (ii) *aen dei figa, get sambadi <u>fo</u> push dem* 'and they figured there'd be someone <u>to</u> encourage them' (unrealized event: complement introduced by *fo*) (1986: 24).

5 A system whereby *relative clauses* are not necessarily introduced by a relativizer, as in HCE *da gai (Ø) gon lei da vainil for mi bin kwot mi prais* 'the guy <u>who</u> is going to lay the vinyl for me had quoted me a price'. In non-relative clauses, *subject-copying* (typically repeating the subject NP with a relevant pronoun form) will often occur, as in HCE *jaepan gaiz <u>dei</u> no giv a haeng, do* 'Japanese guys, <u>they</u> don't give a hang, though' = 'Japanese guys don't give a hang though' (1986: 24).

6 A system of negation in which non-specific subject NPs and constituents of Verb Phrases (VPs) are negated, along with the verb itself. This leads to multiple negation, as in GC <u>non</u> *dag* <u>na</u> *bait* <u>non</u> *kyat* 'no dog bit any cat' (Bickerton 1986: 66).

7   A system in which the *existential* (as in 'there is') and *possession* (as in 'have') are expressed in a similar manner, as in:

GC
dem get	*wan uman we*		*get*	*gyal-pikni*
'there is	a woman who		has	a daughter'
(*existential*)			(*possessive*)	

Haitian French-lexifier creole (HC)
gê	*you*	*fâm*	*ki*	*gê*	*you*	*pitit-fi*
'have	one	woman	who	have	one	daughter'
(*existential*)				(*possessive*)		

(Bickerton 1986: 66)

Trinidad English-lexifier creole (TEC)
it ha' (have)	*a woman*	*who*	*ha'*	*a gyul-chil'*
'there is	a woman	who	has	a daughter'
(*existential*)			(*possessive*)	

8/9 A system whereby the adjective has become a type of stative verb, as in GC *i wiiri* 'he is tired' (Bickerton 1986: 68). Thus, in such instances a *copula* is not required, as in TEC *she marrid* 'she is married'.

10 A system in which there is no subject–verb inversion in yes/no questions, as in GC *i bai di eg-dem* > *i bai di eg-dem?* 'he bought the eggs → did he buy the eggs?' (Bickerton 1986: 70)

11 The use of bimorphemic (two morphemes) *question words*. They are typically compound words derived from the superstratal language, as in GC *wisaid yu bin de?* 'which side [where] have you been' and HC *ki kote ou we pwaso-a?* 'what side [where] did you see the fish?' (1986: 70).

12 The use of *passive equivalents*. The passive voice is extremely rare in creoles and when it does occur, its form is somewhat different from the typical construction, the latter of which is illustrated in the following:

a mosquito$_{agent}$ bit$_{action}$ me $_{affected}$ (active voice) =
I$_{affected}$ was bitten$_{action}$ (by a mosquito)$_{agent}$ (passive voice: *agent* and *affected* are switched; *agent* is no longer obligatory; verb phrase now comprises passive auxiliary + main verb).

In many creoles, the equivalent of the passive voice fronts the *affected* constituent but often gets rid of the *agent* and leaves the verb unchanged, as in:

GC

dem	*a ponish*	*abi*	=
'they (*agent*)	are punishing	us' (*affected*)	=

abi	*a ponish*
'We (*affected*)	are being punished'

Jamaican English-lexifier creole (JEC)

dem	*plaan*	*di trii*	=
'they (*agent*)	planted	the tree' (*affected*)	=

di trii	*plaan*
'the tree (*affected*)	has been planted'.

Since these features are allegedly generated by the bioprogram, some may also be found in non-creole languages as well. Sebba (1997: 175), for example, tells us that English has features 1, 2 and 5; some non-standard varieties, 6. French has feature 7 and many languages have 9 and 10. Scots has 11, and African languages such as Malinke and Kongo have 6 and 11 (Singh 1997). However, to be categorized as a creole, a language would have to have most, if not all, of these 12 features.

The Language Bioprogram Hypothesis (LBH) was a novel approach to the question of creole genesis: it had roots in Chomsky's controversial **Language Acquisition Device**, drew on theories of language acquisition, generated an inventory of classic creole features, suggested that a pidgin was not always an integral part of a creole's life-cycle, proposed that the grammatical similarities 'true' creoles share are not due to a common ancestor (such as WAPP) and speculated on the workings of the human brain in situations that are impossible to test (since the formation environments of extant creoles are long since gone) and difficult to recreate. Not surprisingly, it has generated a great deal of criticism (see Sebba 1997: 178–81 for a more detailed discussion). For example, it is very difficult to test the validity of the LBH with more than just 'classically catastrophic' creoles, all of which in turn need to be identified as a potential data base. However, creoles generally do not have well-documented histories, making it difficult to ascertain factors such as the make-up of the population, whether there was a pidgin that stabilized and whether a creole did actually emerge with a young generation of speakers. Aitchison (1983) in fact criticizes Bickerton for confining his test cases to two creoles that he knows well, namely HCE and GC. This, however, may be somewhat harsh: given the limits of time, money and ability we would be hard-pressed to find linguists (and indeed other professionals) who had extensive knowledge of all the data in their field. Furthermore, in the style of many linguists, Bickerton does make reference to the work of other creolists; drawing on data from languages such as Papiamentu, Haitian French-lexifier creole, Saramaccan, Sranan, Jamaican English-lexifier creole, Mauritian creole and Criolu.

Bickerton has also been accused of constructing a circular argument with the LBH: the existence of the bioprogram is assumed; this bioprogram generates 'classic creole' features; the presence of these features in classic creoles is then taken as evidence of the reality of the bioprogram. Such appraisals are inevitable to an extent since, as previously stated, it is impossible to deliberately recreate and test the conditions of linguistic evolution. However, they may be diffused by reference to other cases where language has been 'reconstituted' because 'the normal generation-to-generation transmission of input data [has been] interrupted or distorted by extralinguistic forces' (Muysken and Bickerton 1988: 282). One such example (outlined below) was recently brought to light in Nicaragua, where members of the country's deaf community have formulated contact sign languages of varying stages of complexity.

In 1979, when the Sandanistas came to power after the Nicaraguan Revolution, they discovered in Managua (on the Pacific side of the island), a long-ignored sector of the community: the deaf population, for whom no provision had ever been made and who consequently lived their lives surrounded by the hearing. These deaf individuals had no homogenous sign language and were instead 'home-signers': each person worked out a system that enabled them to communicate with the hearing people in their immediate environment. Among the Sandanista reforms was the establishment of vocational centres in Managua for deaf teenagers. For many of the students, these centres provided the first point of contact with others like themselves. In the early 1980s, 50 students attended one of these schools. They could not hear, read, talk or lip-read and had no sign language in common, but they rapidly began to communicate with each other, developing a system of signing that their teachers (who initially had had difficulty following the individual home-signs) simply could not follow. Judy Kegl (Rutgers University), who was sent in to help, found that these young adults were signing together but that there was extreme idiolectal variation – there was 'no predictable grammar, no pattern to the way the signs fitted together' (Horizon 1997). When the school had brought this group, this first generation of signers (G1), together they had **koineized** their individual home-signs into a system of shared signs. However, this system was very basic (incorporating only what they had in common), and was heavily influenced by each signer's individual system, hence the variation in its usage. What they had created was the early stage of a pidgin: a jargon.

Kegl also visited a primary school in Managua, where deaf children had come together at a much earlier age than the teenagers in the vocational centre. She noticed in particular a young girl called Mayela who, with her friends, was signing fluently and very differently from the G1 signers. She felt, on seeing Mayela, that 'somebody [had given] this woman the rule book'. Interestingly, the children in this second generation of signers (G2) had *not* been taught to sign; their teachers tried instead to teach them to speak, write and lip-read. Mayela later stated that, outside of lessons, she and her deaf friends had watched older signers and learnt from them. However, Mayela was not conscious that the G2 signers had actually developed the jargon signing they had observed; they had turned it into a grammatical language that they used fluently and confidently: something very much like a creole.

Over the years, Kegl and her assistants recorded most of the Nicaraguan deaf community and were able to observe the differences in language use between the generations. She used a Czech cartoon, 'Mr Koumal', which has no oral component, as the basis of her data. Deaf individuals were shown the cartoon and asked to repeat the story (thus eliciting grammatical constructions) back to a video camera. Kegl found crucial differences between the signing of G1 and G2 members. One such contrast, for example, was in the area of *objectification*. In one of the stories, Mr Koumal has been reduced to begging by the side of the road, and a rich, passing motorist tosses him a coin. In the telling of that last action, G1 signers do not *objectify* the coin; that is, they do not sign 'flat, round object'. Instead, they mimic the trajectory of the coin, so that the bunched fingers of the left hand, for example, are arced through the air to land in the palm of the right. G2 and younger signers sign 'flat, round object', show it has been thrown by making a flicking movement over the shoulder, and then in a separate gesture, the 'flat, round object' sign is shown having landed in the palm of the hand. Overall, G1 signers have mainly an iconic system: their signs are basic and not knitted together with very much grammatical glue. Consequently, their rendition of the story is akin to 'man begs; near road; car drives by; man in car; man throws something; lands in hand'. However, the youngest signer, Barney, a pre-pubescent boy who has grown up with other signers, packs more detail into his signing, which is 'chock full of complexity and structure' (Judy Kegl, Horizon 1997). For this youngster, such fluency is completely natural and done without a second thought, just as most of us speak our native language seemingly effortlessly.

The next question to occupy Kegl and her team was determining where the fluency of the G2 signers had come from. Members of the hearing community in Managua use many gesticulations in their speech, and some of the deaf signs correspond to these. Was it therefore possible that the G2 signers had simply extended the signs they saw around them? Kegl investigated this by testing the proficiency of the hearing community in understanding G2 deaf signs. Her team found that though some signs were understood, the majority were not. They concluded that the gestures G2 signers had seen may have contributed only a few lexical items to their system, but not the bulk of it and definitely not the grammar. The obvious conclusion was that the children had created it.

The Nicaraguan case does seem to have given rise to data complentary to work on the bioprogram. Both G1 and G2 signers were born into an environment of *abnormal transmission* (see Chapter 1, Section 1.3.1); namely to hearing parents who could only provide 'degenerate input' for their children's acquisition of a more suitable language. G1 signers, brought together as teenagers, managed to develop a highly variable, rudimentary system of signing, whereas G2 signers, a community from early childhood, observed this jargon signing and generated a complex, rule-governed, shared language in which they were natively fluent. This would also seem to suggest, as Bickerton has (and Chomsky before him), that there is a critical threshold for language acquisition. Kegl in fact found additional evidence for this. In 1994, she discovered that the deaf on the Atlantic side of the island existed in a pre-Revolution situation: in hearing communities and families, isolated from other deaf, and so were merely home-signers. Without others to sign with (and the presence of a community would seem to be essential in linguistic evolution) they would remain virtually 'language-less'. In 1995, she and helpers set up a school for these home-signers. The students are taught official Nicaraguan Sign Language (NSL) in mixed-age groups and, perhaps as a consequence of this, no new language has been created. The learning pattern that has emerged, however, is still interesting: young children are learning NSL more rapidly than the older signers.

Language acquisition theory has in fact postulated that the years 0–7 are crucial for linguistic development. Between the ages of 8–15 and from 15 onwards, it becomes increasingly more difficult to achieve fluency in a language. This would seem to be borne out in the Nicaraguan case by Ansuelo, who was 16 when he started learning NSL and 2 years later, was competent enough to help in teaching other students. However he will never be better than 'a talented teenager learning a foreign language' (Horizon 1997). Adela, on the other hand, began NSL when she was 4 and is expected to grow up a fully fluent signer.

The ability of the Nicaraguan signers to make up, partially or wholly, for the lack of normal language transmission does tantalizingly point in the direction of the bioprogram. Other work on sign language acquisition (Deuchar 1987; see Romaine 1988) where on the whole, the deaf child receives inadequate input from hearing carers yet develops a signing system, has shown that the latter shares certain features with creoles, such as the use of adjectives as verbs and a lack of copulas and passive constructions. However, Sebba (1997: 272) points out that despite the inadequate input of their immediate carers, such children (unlike those in a creole-formation environment, who have no comparable linguisitc aid) are not necessarily isolated from others who can sign, which inevitably helps in their acquisition of sign language. On the other hand, the Nicaraguan case has been unique in that it may have brought us as close as possible to witnessing the kind of linguistic evolution that may have been pertinent to creole birth. G1 signers, like the first adult slaves on a New World plantation, for example, were deliberately brought together into a community where an instinctive need to communicate evolved. G2 signers, like the first generation of slave children, really had no other linguistic role models than these jargon-using adults. Such cases, though rare, may therefore prove beneficial to the study of creole genesis and more generally, to theories of linguistic evolution.

Another criticism levelled at the LBH is that some 'classic creoles' do not in fact seem to have the expected bioprogram features. Unserdeutsch is one such, having emerged from an unstable jargon within the space of one generation, among indigenous New Guinean students at a German-run boarding school. Yet it displays only four of the expected bioprogram features, whereas Tok Pisin (not a 'classically catastrophic creole'; see pages 52 and 56) surprisingly displays eight. It is possible that since Unserdeutsch emerged from a group that continued to use its native language, the latter served as a

linguistic model for the new creole, thus subjugating the specifica-
tions of the bioprogram. However, the high occurrence of bioprogram features in a tongue such as Tok Pisin, which is, allegedly,
'culturally distanced' from the bioprogram, is difficult to explain.
Nevertheless, even Bickerton admitted that the 12-feature list is not
infallible, and as Sebba (1997: 175) points out:

> this is not only not surprising, it is inevitable, as all languages
> change and creoles, which usually remain in contact with other
> languages, are more likely than the average language to change
> rapidly. Therefore, even if exceptions to 'the twelve' are rela-
> tively easy to find, we would need to check historical evidence
> to see whether they have always been exceptions.

However, as previously stated, that historical evidence is not always
forthcoming.

It is noteworthy that Bickerton's is not the only extant checklist:
Taylor (1971), Markey (1982) and Muysken and Veestra (1994) (all
cited in Sebba 1997: 175), for example, have also put together lists of
characteristic creole features, some of which overlap with the alleged
output of the language bioprogram. As Sebba (1997: 175) points out,
'this shows that there is, in fact, broad agreement that creole languages show similarities to each other ... *and* that there is a fair
amount of agreement about what these similarities are'.

It has also been argued that the conditions Bickerton presupposes
for the bioprogram to kick in do not tally with 'the social and historical realities of creole formation' (Sebba 1997: 179). For example,
Bickerton assumes that for the formation of a classic creole to have
taken place, quite a few children would have had to have been produced very quickly, before the jargon of the adults had time to stabilize. However, it is highly likely that in 'classic creole'-formation
environments such as plantations where slaves existed in dehuman-
izing conditions, birth rates were quite low and child mortality rates
quite high. Thus, the 'jump' from unstable jargon to fully fledged
creole may have taken longer than the space of one generation. In
addition, Bickerton (1981: 5) has also been criticized for assuming
that any children who were born into and survived in these communities had no real language model other than the 'degenerate input'
of this unstable jargon, since the use of the native languages of the
adult community was deliberately oppressed or marginalized so
much so that they were 'receding rapidly into the past' (1981: 5).
Bickerton's presupposition was doubtless based on historical

accounts of the slave trade and of the set-up of New World planta-tions, which often state that planters forcibly prohibited the use of the slaves' native languages. Whether or not this is true, we can only really speculate about what actually occurred in the slave barracks. Thus Bickerton, in assuming that such prohibitions extended into the intimate but highly stressful relationship between adult slave carer and slave child is not necessarily any more (or less) wrong than those who assume that the adult slave carer would naturally have used their native tongue. However, as Sebba (1997: 180) points out, it does impact on the theory of how the bioprogram works. If chil-dren in these communities had only the rudimentary jargon to work with, then the relevant issues surround monolingual first language (creole) acquisition. On the other hand, if they were exposed to at least one substratal language as well, then what becomes relevant is the question of how acquiring the latter (a fully fledged language) impacts on the generation of a new (creole) one. If this were the case, then it is likely that children drew on the ready-made substratal models rather than their bioprogram for features of creole grammar. This possibility therefore suggests that certain characteristic creole features are not in fact bioprogram-generated, but are instead a sub-stratal inheritance – a claim that has in fact been made (see, for example, Sebba (1997: 182–90) and Arends *et al.* (1995: Chapter 9) who illustrate the case for substratal influence in the generation of creole grammar).

It is noteworthy though that claims of influence from either parental language group continuously engender debate and controversy, pos-sibly because in corresponding to or challenging established modes of thought, such assertions often have wider implications. Thus, as stated on page 38, early classifications of pidgins and creoles defined them as bastardized versions of European languages, a conclusion that grew out of a wider, racist presumption about the intellectual and cultural inferiority of Africans (which of course legitimized the slave trade). When the Herskovitses stated that the creoles they had investigated showed heavy substratal influence, it was not only a turning point for creole enquiry but was also indicative of a new perspective that sought to finally recognize and validate the contribution of Africa to New World culture. As Alleyne (1980: 2) states:

> the study of ... 'creole' languages ... has ... taken on new dimensions and a new significance, having become involved in the social, cultural and political conflicts of our times ... issues

such as the structure of the Black family, the 'soul' mystique, the religious expression, and the linguistic expression of Black people are being raised both in the academic world and on the political front. Black culture or modes of behaviour ... are no longer sources of embarrassment or feelings of insecurity when compared with corresponding White modes of behaviour.

Theories such as monogenesis were formulated against such a background and the collapse of Empire was played out in the linguistic arena: the touted importance of substratal languages in creole formation marginalized that of Europe's tongues. Creolists appeared to have become divided into two camps: *sostratomani*, 'substratomaniacs', and *sostratofobi*, 'substratophobes' (terms coined by Hall in 1955; cited in Holm 1988: 43). The battlefield became dominated by accusations of subscribing to the *Cafeteria Principle*, a term coined by Dillard (1970) to explain the once unquestioned belief that creoles, in the main, comprised linguistic bits and pieces from the dialects of the superstratal population. Some substratists were similarly criticized for claiming, also on the grounds of mere resemblances, substratal ancestry for certain creole features. According to Bickerton (1981: 49):

> if it is absurd to suppose that a creole could mix fragments of Irish, Wessex, Norfolk, and Yorkshire dialects, it is at least as absurd to suppose that a creole could mix fragments of Yoruba, Akan, Igbo, Mandinka, and Wolof – to mention some of the African languages which substratomaniacs frequently invoke. ... One would think that the first task in constructing any substratum theory would be to show that the necessary groups were in the necessary places at the necessary times. But this simply has not been done.

In addition, Bickerton felt that substratists should explain *why* a creole would inherit a particular rule:

> Let us suppose that a very common structure in Caribbean creoles is also attested for Yoruba and perhaps one or two other relatively minor languages. ... To most substratomaniacs, the mere existence of such similarities constitutes self-evident proof of the connection. They seldom even consider the problem of transmission. How does a rule get from Yoruba into a creole? ... Nobody can deny that, in every case, there were many other African languages involved in each area. ... What could be so

special about a particular Yoruba rule ... that would cause it to be accepted over all competitors in a number of different and quite separate groups?

(Bickerton 1981: 48, 50)

Bickerton's comments 'raised the temperature of the debate without necessarily improving its quality' (Sebba 1997: 181) but they also provided serious food for thought: Bickerton's stance made it clear that (socio)linguistic issues had to be resolved by recourse to (socio)linguistic data. In other words, it was simply inadequate to accept explanations because they conformed to a particular world view. In the study of languages born in obscurity, cultural clashes and the oppression of the powerless (factors that are clearly politi- cally loaded) creolists had to be able to objectively justify their analyses as far as possible. Hence research into both super- and sub- stratal inheritances has sought to become more rigorous, balanced and structured. Work is also continuing in the field of language acquisition and into what may constitute the grammar universal to us all. These different lines of enquiry all feed into each other. For example, if a creole and its superstratal parent share feature X, it may be a case of inheritance. If feature X was also significant in the substrata, then reinforcement may have come into play: it passed into the creole because its presence in both parent groups strength- ened its chance of survival. Yet if feature X can be shown to be common to many seemingly unrelated languages, then its presence in the creole may be primarily due to directions from the biopro- gram (and may have been strengthened by its presence in one or more of the parent languages).

Carrington (1992: 341) has observed, however, that while work into language acquisition and bioprogram features is exciting and has obvious merits, potentially useful creole data is fast disappearing because linguists have, in a manner of speaking, jumped in at the deep end:

Unlike the now conventional thrust towards the discovery of UG [Universal Grammar] in which the study of the mechanisms of some languages appears to be providing insights into its nature, in the current state of pidgin/creole studies there appears to be a mechanism of premature feedback that is inhibiting the description of the creole languages themselves in favor of the speculative exploitation of their salient characteristics. This statement does not deny that there is some significant descriptive study taking place, but it is a challenge to scholars to be prepared to delay their gratification and to study pidgins and creoles per se, rather than hasten to guess at UG before the requisite data has been assembled.

Nevertheless, investigation into issues of pidgin and creole genesis is on-going, and Crowley (1991: 385) believes that, eventually, creolists may agree that such contact languages, which are undoubtedly formed in radical circumstances, contain 'a set of features combining substratum and superstratum features, as well as other features that develop independently, for a variety of reasons, including universal pressures'. The field is not yet at such a harmonious stage, but exploration along different paths may eventually lead to one such destination. If this is the case, then 'the ultimate theory of creolization ... may have to be as much of a creole as the language it describes' (Singh 1991: 4).

Endnotes

1. In addition to using the FT processes discussed, speakers will sometimes adopt strategies such as loud speech, supplementary gestures and diminutive usages. The combination of these with features such as repetition and simplified vocabulary has resulted in the alternative label *Baby Talk Theory*.
2. Valdman (1981, cited in Arends *et al.* 1995: 97) argued that the social status of the non-native speaker is a crucial factor in determining which strategies are used. Speech addressed to low-status foreigners will often draw on conventions such as imitation and telegraphic condensation, while that addressed to foreigners accorded a high status often relies on accommodation strategies.

|3|

An' den de news spread across de lan'
The creole continuum

3.1 Introduction

In the last chapter, we looked at some of the theories of how pidgins and creoles come into existence. As we have seen, one of the pre-suppositions they all share is the fact that such languages emerge out of a particular type of language contact. However, once they develop into native languages, creoles (and extended pidgins) often continue to exist in a multilingual context that is also home to their original lexical source language, or lexifier.[1] For example, Tok Pisin co-exists with English as well as the indigenous languages of New Guinea. In the Caribbean (as stated in Chapter 1), Trinidad's English-lexifier creole co-exists not only with a French-lexifier cre-ole, Bhojpuri and Chinese (albeit each used by a minority of speak-ers) but also with English, the now official and ex-superstratal language of the island.

Thus, language contact often continues throughout a creole's life, and in this chapter we shall be particularly concerned with one of the outcomes of contact with lexical source languages: the emergence of the *creole continuum*.

3.2 The creole continuum

In territories where creoles and their respective ex-superstratal lan-guages are used, there is often differentiation (in terms of prestige) between the two. Even though a creole may be the mother tongue of the majority of a population, it will not necessarily be imbued with any great measure of status in that speech community; whereas the ex-superstratal language, used by a small but elite sector and institutionalized as an official tongue, may be seen as highly prestigious. This type of linguistic co-existence is not uncommon and can produce, depending on the particulars of each situation, diverse outcomes. One result, for example, can be a type of language death known as *language murder*, or loss of a less prestigious language as speakers increasingly favour one with more social status. Gal (1979; one of the earliest studies in this area) observed this phenomenon in the village of Oberwart in the Burgenland of eastern Austria. The village, founded about a thousand years ago, had existed for a substantial period of time as a Hungarian-speaking community. Between 1200–1600, however, German migrants moved into Oberwart, certain sectors of which eventually became bilingual. The village was granted to Austria in 1921, at which time 75 per cent of the population spoke Hungarian. In 1971, however, only 25 per cent, all with 'peasant roots', did (McMahon 1994: 292). The majority of the population had shifted to German. Why?

The nineteenth century had seen great changes in Oberwart: the small, peasant village began to evolve into a thriving city through an influx of wealthy, Lutheran, German-speaking merchants and artisans. In addition, the area also attracted Catholic Hungarian-speaking professionals in the latter half of the nineteenth century; and the co-existence of these two influential groups resulted in the retention of German as a dominant language in the Lutheran community and the adoption of Hungarian as the language of professionals and of higher education. The twentieth century, however, brought a change in the fortunes of both languages. When Oberwart was granted to Austria, the Hungarian elite migrated to Hungary, and the Hungarian speakers who stayed behind were mainly peasants. Political ties with Hungary gradually became loosened, and more and more German monolinguals settled in the community. As such, Hungarian gradually lost prestige and German conversely became the dominant language in more and more contexts, and is continuing to do so. The peasant population has since also become bilingual, and 'Hungarian is now a mark of peasant identity or peasant ancestry ... [and] is used predominantly in in-group usage, among people with a high degree of peasantness' (McMahon 1994: 293). German, on the other hand, is seen as the language of progress and of a more prosperous future; indeed, 'parents are proud if their children speak

German with no Hungarian influence' (McMahon 1994: 292). As such, Hungarian in Oberwart is considered a dying language (though it continues to thrive elsewhere, as in Hungary) and German, in accordance with the terminology of the field, is its murderer.

One of the distinguishing characteristics of language murder is that the languages involved are not closely related, if at all. In addition, the structure of the dying language is not necessarily affected by its co-existence with the prestigious language; in other words, the former does not always 'borrow dominant language structures, and may not even follow patterns in the dominant language' (McMahon 1994: 291). However, in another type of language death, *language suicide*, the two languages *are* related, and the one with less prestige borrows and absorbs structures from that with high status. The less prestigious language therefore 'commits suicide' by ingesting features 'alien' to its system.

Language suicide studies have mostly taken place in creole-speaking communities, in some of which (as we shall see), certain creole speakers take on lexical and grammatical features from the ex-superstratal languages. It is noteworthy, though, that this is not always the case: a creole and its ex-superstratal language can sometimes exist side-by-side without any real linguistic interchange taking place. In Haiti, for example, a French-lexifier creole (HFC) is used with French in what is often described as a situation of *diglossia* (see, for example, Sebba 1997). French, as the language with high status (H), is used in areas that are considered important and prestigious, such as administration, law, education and literary writing. HFC, on the other hand, is the language with low prestige (L) and is consequently restricted to everyday, largely informal use. In diglossic situations, speakers generally assume that the L language is unsuited to 'higher' functions, and therefore tend to be reluctant (or completely opposed) to extending it into the domains of the H language. As we shall see in Chapter 4, this has indeed been one of the major problems that have plagued attempts to 'elevate' HFC, especially in the educational arena.

In Haiti, a small elite is bilingual in HFC and French, but the bulk of the population is monolingual in the creole. It is perhaps as a consequence of this, in addition to the sharp differentiation of function between the two languages, that language suicide has not taken place. In other words, most HFC speakers cannot incorporate French structures into their creole because they simply have little or no knowledge of the latter language; and members of the bilingual

population keep their use of the two languages separate, thus
preventing any interchange between them.

However, as mentioned on page 71, interaction between a creole
and its lexical source language *does* sometimes take place; with
speakers of the former generally taking on features of the latter. This
language suicide is not wholesale: the creole does not simply get
'devoured by its parent' (Aitchison 1981: 210) in one tremendous
gulp, leaving the entire speech community with the ex-superstratal
language as its only linguistic resource. Instead, varieties that combine features of the creole and its one-time lexifier emerge, and come
to exist as stable lects in the speech community.

This is the case in places such as Jamaica, which has an English-
lexifier creole (JEC) that co-exists with English (specifically a standard form of English) as an official language. These two are
completely different languages, as can be seen in JEC *mi a nyam* and
standard English (stE) *I am eating*. They differ lexically (JEC uses
nyam where stE uses *eat*; morphologically (JEC uses *mi* vs stE *I*); and
syntactically (JEC uses *a nyam* which signals present habitual aspect,
as opposed to stE present tense of *to be (am)* + main verb-*ing (eating)*). However, varieties or lects that combine the two to differing
extents are also in evidence, as in *me a eat, me eatin', I eatin', I is
eatin'* (Sebba 1997: 210). These lects are thought to be ranged on a
creole continuum, which evolves when

> a creole coexists with its lexical source language and there is a
> social motivation for the creole speaker to acquire the standard,
> so that the speech of individuals takes on features of the latter –
> or avoids features of the former – to varying degrees.
>
> (Holm 1988: 52).

The creole continuum model was first devised by DeCamp (1971)
and applied to Jamaica, which he termed a '*post-creole* speech community' (DeCamp 1971: 351); a categorization which encapsulates
the idea that the continuum is a later stage of a creole's life cycle,
developing after it has been firmly established as a native language.
However, DeCamp clearly stated that the emergence of a *post-creole
continuum* is contingent upon two primary factors.

1 The dominant official language of the community must be the
  standard language corresponding to the creole.

Thus, for a post-creole continuum to emerge in a community with an
English-lexifier creole, for example, the creole must co-exist with

standard English as an institutionalized language. The latter inevitably carries social prestige (as the language of education, administration, religion and so on) and, as such, exerts 'corrective pressure' (1971: 351) on creole speakers who want to, and are able to, acquire proficiency in it.

2 The formerly rigid social stratification must have *partially* (not completely) broken down.

Slave societies such as those once extant in islands like Trinidad and Jamaica operated with a strict division between European and African, powerful and powerless. However, after Emancipation (authorized in British colonies in 1836), these societies evolved into ones where opportunities for education and social mobility arose (in varying degrees) for some, not all, native creole speakers. Thus, the 'corrective pressure' of the standard across the community would not have been homogenous. For example, it would have had no effect on a farmer in a rural, relatively isolated village where there was neither the opportunity nor motivation to participate in even the most elementary level of schooling. There are in fact still villages like this in rural Trinidad, where children whose families have little or no money for necessary school supplies attend school sporadically until the age of 10–11 (when the law requires them to complete the Common Entrance Exam for entry into high school) and then drop out to work full-time with their labourer parents. However, for those who complete primary, secondary and/or tertiary education (processes which bring them into contact with urban centres where the language of work and many leisure activities is the standard), their access to, and perhaps motivation to acquire, the standard increases in direct proportion to their educational level.

The emergence of the continuum depends upon this non-uniformity of 'corrective pressure' from the standard: if all native creole speakers had unlimited access to the standard, and were all motivated to the same degree to acquire it, it is more likely that the creole would simply be abandoned for the more prestigious and 'progessive' option. Instead, the continuum emerges because 'acculturative influences impinge on different speakers with varying degrees of effectiveness, drawing some of them more than others toward the standard. The degree of acculturation varies with such factors as age, poverty, and isolation from urban centres' (DeCamp 1971: 351).

Thus, in places such as Jamaica, DeCamp (1971: 350) believed that:

there is no sharp cleavage between creole and standard. Rather there is a linguistic continuum, a continuous spectrum of speech varieties ranging from the 'bush talk' of Quashie to the educated standard of Philip Sherlock [then principal of the Mona campus at the University of the West Indies] and Norman Manley [then Prime Minister of Jamaica]. ... Each Jamaican speaker commands a span of this continuum, the breadth of the span depending on the breadth of his social contacts; a labor leader, for example, commands a greater span of varieties than does a suburban middle-class housewife.

Using the Jamaican examples on page 72, this continuum can be visualized as follows:

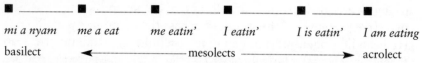

mi a nyam	me a eat	me eatin'	I eatin'	I is eatin'	I am eating
basilect	←————————————— mesolects ————————————→				acrolect

At one end is the *basilect*, which is the variety that is most creole-like, typically spoken by those who are at the bottom of the socio-economic ladder and so have the least access to institutions such as education and therefore to the standard. At the opposite end is the *acrolect*, the local variety of standard English, which is generally used by the society's elite: the well-educated, well-off professionals. Sebba (1997: 212) states that in Jamaica, this variety is only marginally different from British standard English (BstE) in morphology, grammar and lexicon (apart from vocabulary items which denote local flora, fauna and foodstuffs). However, the acrolect shares many phonological features with the basilect, and so could be termed 'standard English with a Jamaican accent' (1997: 212). This is similar to the situation in other islands of the Anglophone Caribbean. For example, in Trinidad, the local acrolect is virtually identical to current British standard English apart from certain morphological and grammatical constructs (such as the use of *gotten*, a fossilization of an older English past participle; and the lack of inversion in questions, as in *you see my books anywhere?*). In terms of lexicon, the Trinidad acrolect has incorporated items for place names, flora, fauna, foodstuffs, religious celebrations, local customs and local mythology from the island's Amerindian, Spanish, French, African and East Indian settlers. It has also come to include natively coined vocabulary and, in the latter half of this century, has increasingly absorbed items from North American

English. A good example of this lexical mix can be seen in the following opening from 'Pride of a Lion' (*Trinidad Express*, 13 July 1999):

> *Mamaguying* friends have been *kidding* me about *putting goat-mouth* on Roaring Lion [a local calypso singer] simply because I was celebrating his 'Caroline' [his latest calypso] last week just days before his death, as if the man wasn't an ailing 91 with Mr. Death hovering around waiting for the slip and then the slide that is the lot of all of us.

> *mamaguy* = 'to tease'; *mamaguying* 'teasing' (local coinage)
> *kidding* = American English 'to joke with'
> *putting goat-mouth* = 'to bring bad luck to someone' (local coinage)

As the example makes clear, the majority of the lexicon none the less consists of items mutually intelligible with British standard English.

In terms of phonology, the acrolect and basilect continue to have a great deal in common, such as the use of /t/ where BstE has /θ/, as in *tunda~thunder*; /d/~/ð/, as in *fada~father*; /ɛ/~/a/, as in *heng~hang*. The acrolect here too can therefore be said to be fundamentally standard English with a Trinidadian accent.

In between the polar opposites of the basilect and acrolect are the varieties that mix the two to varying degrees: the *mesolects*. These are a continuous range of lects, and their speakers will be more or less creole- or standard-like, depending on their individual access to, and identification with, the basilect or acrolect.

As stated on page 72, DeCamp saw the continuum as the next stage of a pidgin→creole life cycle, with the creole slowly and eventually merging with its lexical source language. Thus in this framework, the lects (in particular, the mesolects) represent 'a filling in of the linguistic space between creole and standard language' (Rickford 1987: 32) and, simultaneously, reflect 'the filling in of the social space between highest and lowest castes of colonial society after Emancipation' (1987: 32). However, DeCamp stated that even though sociological factors such as age, level of education, occupation, income and so on correlated with the linguistic variation on the continuum, the latter should be based solely on linguistic data (which resulted in a linear model as on page 74) so that it could be interpreted without 'circularity of reasoning'; that is, it avoids conclusions such as 'words characteristic of high school graduates are commonly used by high school graduates' (DeCamp 1961: 82; quoted in Holm 1988: 56). We shall examine DeCamp's notion of the continuum more closely in Section 3.3.

3.2.1 *The implicational hierarchy*

Even though, as I have argued, the mesolects can be classified as varieties that combine features from the creole and the standard official language, these mixtures are not random. Let us, for example, abstract a continuum for Trinidad (to vary the illustration somewhat!). A basilectal utterance could be *me na bax she*, the standard English equivalent of which is *I didn't hit her*. Mesolectal possibilities include *me no box she, me no did box she, I didn't box/hit she, I didn't box her*; but not **me na bax her*, **I na bax her*, **I no did box her*. Why should this be?

DeCamp (1971) stated that the mixtures present in mesolects are caused by an *implicational hierarchy*. In other words, the occurrence of linguistic feature X in a speaker's usage necessarily implies or indicates the presence of feature Y in her idiolect as well. Thus, if we look back at our Trinidad example, a speaker who uses *mi* as a first person singular subject pronoun is unlikely to use *her* as a third person singular object pronoun. A speaker who uses *I* and *her* in these respective cases will, in all probability, use the more standard [ɒ], instead of [a] in the pronunciation of *box*; or, even more probably, will substitute the standard *hit*.

DeCamp (1971: 355) illustrated implicational scaling with a minicontinuum based on data from seven informants interviewed in a survey of 142 Jamaican speech communities. Six features (see Table 3.1) were selected as being the most salient 'among the many that define the continuum of Jamaican English'.

Table 3.1 Features

Acrolectal usages		Basilectal usages	
+A	child	−A	pikni
+B	eat	−B	nyam
+C	/θ/ ~ /t/	−C	/t/
+D	/ð/ ~ /d/	−D	/d/
+E	granny	−E	nana
+F	didn't	−F	no ben/did

Source: after DeCamp (1971: 355)

The use of [+] features indicates a speaker's more acrolectal usages and [–], those that are more basilectal. Thus, a speaker who is graded as [+] A, B and E makes habitual use of such standard vocabulary items, while a speaker evaluated with [–] A, B and E uses the creole alternatives. Similarly, a speaker with [+] C and D maintains the standard English distinction in the pronunciation of word pairs such as *thin~tin* and *then~den*; while these merge into *tin* and *den* for a [–] C and D speaker. Finally, a [+] F speaker will use a standard construction (auxiliary past tense *did* + contracted negative marker *n't*) in negative past tense constructions, whereas a [–] F speaker will use a creole alternative: negative marker *no* + tense marker *been (ben)* or *did*. DeCamp found that his informants used the features listed in Table 3.1 in the following ways.

Table 3.2 Speakers' usage

Speaker	Occurrence of features					
1	+A	+B	+C	–D	+E	+F
2	–A	+B	–C	–D	+E	+F
3	–A	+B	–C	–D	–E	–F
4	–A	–B	–C	–D	–E	–F
5	+A	+B	+C	+D	+E	+F
6	+A	+B	–C	–D	+E	+F
7	–A	+B	–C	–D	+E	–F

Source: after DeCamp (1971: 355)

We can see very clearly that, according to this analysis, Speaker 4 (who has [–] values for all six features) has the most creole-like speech and is therefore the most basilectal; while Speaker 5 (who has all [+] values) is the most acrolectal. The other speakers, who fall in between these two extremes in various combinations, are therefore mesolectal.

If we look a bit more closely at the mesolectal patterns, we can see evidence of DeCamp's implicational hierarchy. Take, for example, the pattern of usage for features A and B. Three speakers, 1, 5 and 6, have the pattern [+A, +B] *child, eat*; 2, 3 and 7 have [–A, +B] *pikni, eat*; and speaker 4, [–A, –B] *pikni, nyam*. The fourth permutation, [+A, –B] *child, nyam* does not occur. DeCamp (1971: 356) maintains that this is not just down to chance: if a speaker uses *child*, it implies that they will use *eat* and not *nyam*, since the latter 'is a word much further down the social scale than is *pikni*, much more a shibboleth of Quashie speech. Any speaker of sufficient social status and in a sufficiently formal speech situation to say *child* instead of *pikni* would normally not say *nyam*.' The usage pattern of features A and B also implies something about the usage of the other lexical feature E. If speakers use *child* and *eat*, it is highly likely that they will also use *granny*. This is in fact true of the [+A, +B] speakers 1, 5 and 6. In addition, we might make an intuitive guess that if a speaker uses acrolectal lexical items, then they will also use acrolectal grammatical forms. Again, this holds true: Speakers 1, 5 and 6 all have [+A, +B, +E, +F] patterns.

A similar implicational pattern is apparent with features C and D. Speaker 5 has a [+C, +D] pattern, Speaker 1 [+C, −D], and Speakers 2, 3, 4, 6 and 7 [−C, −D]. The pattern [−C, +D] does not occur. This implies that if a speaker contrasts /ð/~/d/, as in *then~den*, she will also maintain a /θ/~/t/ contrast, distinguishing words such as *thin~tin*.

Such an interdependency of features is best illustrated in the implicational scale model shown in Table 3.3:

Table 3.3 Implicational scale model

Speaker	Occurrence of features					
	B	E	F	A	C	D
5	+	+	+	+	+	+
1	+	+	+	+	+	−
6	+	+	+	+	−	−
2	+	+	+	−	−	−
7	+	+	−	−	−	−
3	+	−	−	−	−	−
4	−	−	−	−	−	−

At the top is 5, the most acrolectal speaker and at the bottom, basilectal Speaker 4. The mesolectal speakers are arranged between these two poles in such a manner so as to clearly show movement from a more creole- to a more standard-like usage. An implicational ordering of features is also evident: usage of feature [+A] implies usage of [+B, +E, +F]. Usage of [+D] implies usage of [+C]. Notice too that the model bears out the idea expressed in Section 3.2, that acrolectal speakers use a great deal of standard lexical and grammatical features, but can share phonological features with the basilect. For example, with the exception of Speaker 5, Speakers 1 and 6 use the four standard lexical and grammatical features but do not maintain standard English phonological contrasts, in a manner similar or identical to Speaker 4.

DeCamp believed that, once such a continuum of linguistic usage had been constructed, relevant socio-economic information could then be considered:

> We may note, for example, that informant 5, at one end of the line, is a young and well-educated proprietor of a successful radio and appliance shop in Montego Bay; that informant 4, at the other end of the line, is an elderly and illiterate peasant farmer in an isolated mountain village; and that the social and economic facts on the other informants are roughly (not exactly) proportional to these informants' positions on the continuum. For example, informant 6 has had fewer years of formal schooling than has informant 7, but her responsible position as a market clerk gives her a higher income, more social prestige, and more opportunity to observe the speech of educated speakers, and this helps to explain her relative position on the continuum.
>
> (DeCamp 1971: 358)

The continuum model was therefore meant to serve as an analytical tool that could be used to 'calculate' and represent (with supplementary information on the social context of linguistic usage) a type of variation that emerges in some creole-speaking communities. Though it has become well established in creole studies, it has not gone unchallenged. Many linguists have questioned its viability and/or wondered whether it should either be amended in some way, or discarded altogether. We shall explore some of these issues now in Section 3.3.

3.3 Quibbles and queries

Rickford (1987: 15–16) states that the major concerns about the continuum have been the following.

1 Do creole and standard represent discrete and sharply separated categories, or do they represent polar varieties between which there is continuous variation?

2 Is variation in the community unidimensional or multidimensional? That is, can all or most variants and varieties be
  linearly ordered in terms of a single dimension such as
  'creoleness' or 'standardness'?

3 Does the continuum model do justice to the social and stylistic dimensions of linguistic variation?

4 Is it valid to maintain DeCamp's (1971) view of the continuum as an extension of Bloomfield's (1933) life-cycle model –
  first a pidgin, then a creole, then a (post-)creole continuum?

5 Does linguistic variation in putative continuum speech
  communities (such as Guyana, Jamaica and Hawaii) represent
  decreolizing change in progress, that is, movement away from
  creole norms and toward the norms of lexically related standard languages?

We shall now look at each of these issues in the following sub
sections (based on Rickford's 1987 discussion).

3.3.1 Discrete or non-discrete?

As previously stated, the continuum model assumes that the interac
tion of a creole and its lexical source language produces varieties tha
range from the basilect through to the acrolect: 'polar varietie
between which there is continuous variation'. The widespread usag
and acceptance of this paradigm has, to a large extent, 'made it real'
we talk about DeCamp's (post-)creole continuum as if it were 'mimic
king rather than projecting reality' (adapted from Carrington 1992
95). However, it is possible to analyse the variation that exists in
'post-creole speech community' from a different theoretical perspec
tive. For example, where linguists such as Cassidy (1961), Craig (1971
1980) and Rickford (1987) have endorsed a continuum analysis fo
their creole-speaking communities, others from the 'same or simila
communities', such as Tsuzaki (1971), Lawton (1978) and Gibsor
(1982) (all quoted in Rickford 1987: 20) have argued that, in these, ɛ
creole and standard continue to co-exist discretely, or as two com
pletely separate systems. In this model, any intermediate varieties tha
emerge are not structured mixtures of the two (such as mesolects) bu
are instead essentially either the standard with some creole features o
creole with some influence from the standard.

Rickford (1987), however, counters the argument of discreteness or
several grounds, including the fact that even linguists who have resistec

a continuum analysis have either inadvertently acknowledged its existence or appear to be contradicted by the actual language data from those communities. For example, in her analysis of Jamaican English-lexifier creole (JEC), Bailey (1966) adopts the discrete perspective in stating that the creole is 'spoken throughout the island ... *alongside* the officially recognised English' (emphasis mine). She acknowledges, however, that there is 'extensive cross interference' between the two, thus pointing to the existence of mesolects. In Guyana, Allsopp as far back as 1958 had stated that there were at least nine ways of saying something like *I told him*, ranging from this most standard (and thus acrolectal?) version through intermediate (mesolectal?) versions such as *a tel im*, and *a tel ii*, to the most creole (basilectal?) *mi tel am* (Rickford 1987: 18).

One of the most important points that Rickford (1987) makes in defence of a continuum analysis is that if we assume the variation which arises is simply 'standard with incursions from the creole' or vice versa, then we are suggesting that any combination of creole and standard features, or 'random mutual interference' (Bickerton 1973: 64) is possible. As we have seen in Section 3.2.1, this is in fact not the case: mixtures of creole and standard features appear to be structured and non-random, something neatly captured by DeCamp's implicational hierarchy.

It is perhaps important to state here that there is no definitive answer to the question posed in (1) (page 79). Rickford's counter-arguments to a discrete analysis are not meant to lead to the conclusion that because a continuum analysis is an effective model for dealing with the variation that can arise from the mixture of creole and standard, it must necessarily be used in all cases. As we have seen, the situation of contact in different speech communities can have different outcomes, so that a continuum model may be the best mode of representation for 'the gradient creole–standard relation in places such as Grenada and Jamaica' but a 'discrete co-systems model' may be better suited to diglossic communities such as Haiti (Rickford 1987: 22). Thus, both continuum and discrete systems models are viable; it is up to linguists, working from the data, to decide which is most appropriate for individual communities.

3.3.2 *Unidimensional or multidimensional?*

This section deals with questions (2) and (3) together because the issues they cover overlap to an extent, in that they both address the social dimensions of language use. As we saw in Section 3.2, linguistic varieties are organized on a single (uni-)dimension of lects in the continuum model. DeCamp made this decision not only to avoid circularity of reasoning, as stated earlier, but also because he believed that a linear unidimensional continuum was a simple and effective tool for describing linguistic variation, and that the sociolinguistic factors which are often correlated with such a phenomenon were in fact relatively unimportant:

> The amount of linguistic variation [in Jamaica] which is neither a part of the continuum nor a matter of simple word geography [i.e. some lexical items may vary from region to region] is surprisingly small. That is, relatively few features vary with age, sex, occupation, ethnic group etc., except to the extent that these co-variables are themselves part of the continuum; e.g., the very old and the very young tend more towards the creole end of the continuum than do young adults.

(DeCamp 1971: 357)

Linguists who have followed DeCamp's example have been criticized for ignoring or marginalizing such social factors. For example, Le Page (1978: 6; emphasis mine) points out that '*how* a speaker is motivated to move across the continuum' should be just as important as establishing the lects that exist on it. However, Rickford (1987: 31) notes that the criticism in fact applies to the way in which the continuum has been used and not to the continuum itself: some linguists such as Bickerton (1973, 1975) and Day (1973) (both cited in Rickford 1987) treat social factors as secondary data in their continuum analyses whereas others, such as Edwards (1970), Winford (1972) and Rickford (1979) (all cited in Rickford 1987) make them integral to their studies. Rickford maintains that since social factors are considered at some point, this criticism does not invalidate or undermine the continuum model itself:

> The continuum is merely a conceptual/analytical tool, which forces one neither to attend nor to neglect sociopsychological considerations. The 'asocial' criticism may derive in part from the tendency of continuum scholars to work outward from linguistic patterns to the social characteristics of their speakers, rather than vice versa. Whether social characteristics are considered first or last does not in itself reflect their importance in the analysis.

(Rickford 1987: 31)

However, some linguists *have* in fact criticized the continuum model as inadequate in itself. Washabuagh (1977; cited in Rickford 1987), working on data from Providence Island (PI), Colombia, first addressed the possible inadequacy of the unidimensional continuum, since he had found that variation on PI was not only on a vertical axis (that is, moving through basilect, mesolect and acrolect) but also on a theoretical, 'horizontal' axis between careful and casual speech. Thus, not only was there variation between basilectal *fi* 'for' and acrolectal *tu* 'to' as a complementizer (as in *mi wan fi/tu see she* 'I want to see her') but also between 'careful' *fi* and 'casual' *fuh* [fə], both basilectal uses. Bickerton (1977) contended that such careful/casual distinctions did not merit a separate axis, since such pronunciation differences were simply a typical result of rapid speech: word-final stressed vowels are often reduced to schwa in such contexts. Rickford (1987) agrees that a horizontal axis in such cases is unnecessary, but for different reasons. He points out that 'casual' variants are often perceived by native creole speakers as being 'more creole' or basilectal than 'careful' alternatives. In addition, some processes seem to occur more for some speakers than others: Rickford (1980; cited in Rickford 1987: 25) found that in areas with certain English-lexifier creoles, mesolectal speakers closer to the basilectal end of the continuum articulate a habitual aspect marker *does* as *da* more frequently than mid-mesolectal speakers. Thus, 'it is most unlikely that the careful/casual contrast does not involve elements of the acrolectal/basilectal opposition' (Rickford 1987: 25). If this is true, then the careful/casual distinction does not necessitate a separate axis, as it is already subsumed in that between acrolect and basilect.

Abrahams (1983; cited in Rickford 1987), too, contended that a distinction not covered by the unidimensional continuum model was that between the 'sweet talk' and 'broad talk' used in most of the Caribbean. The former is 'a demonstration of the speaker's abilities in Standard English, but strictly on the elaborate oratorical level' (Rickford 1987: 26). A good example of this tradition, albeit in the fictional medium, can be seen in Lovelace's *While Gods are Falling*, a novel set in 1960s' Trinidad. The following excerpt is taken from a love letter that the main character, Saga, has written to a girl he is trying to impress. Lovelace's parody of the 'sweet-talking' tradition brings Saga fairly close to acrolectal usage but highlights the fact that it is not his native lect:

My darling Evangeline, yore beautie is beyond compare in my philoprogenitiveness I seek now to make you acknowledged of the deepness of my emoshun for you which is beyond me to express. There is no other one in my life or in my days or in my nights who I feel such affeckshun for as you that afflick me with such deep and tender passhon so deep and loving when I think of you . . .

(Lovelace 1965: 77)

'Broad talk', on the other hand, is more 'everyday', sharp and 'street-wise', taking the form of witty repartee and *picong* 'insults/jibes' (from Trinidad's English-lexifier creole; derived from French *piquante* 'sharp'). As such, it is predicated on the use of basilectal features. It would therefore seem that, again, since distinctions of 'broad' and 'sweet talk' involve basilectal and acrolectal usage respectively, a separate axis is not a necessary addendum to the continuum.

It must be noted, however, that a linear, unidimensional model is truly inadequate in some contexts. Le Page and Tabouret-Keller (1985), for instance, argue that in a multilingual area such as the Cayo District in Belize, where Spanish, Carib, standard English and an English-lexifier creole co-exist, the linguistic situation is obviously more complicated than that represented by the traditional continuum, which allows only for the interaction of two systems. In addition, such a context makes it extremely clear that social factors, such as the expression of identity, become very important when multilingual speakers make linguistic choices. They say of three informants, MP and GM (both schoolgirls) and OL ('old lady'), who all regarded themselves as speakers of the same creole, that their creole usage was in fact markedly different from each other's, showing varying degrees of influence from the co-extant languages. It would seem therefore 'that each of the three in their linguistic behaviour exhibits the effects of both individual and communal acts of identity, and in doing so they position themselves in multidimensional space' (Le Page 1980: 126–7; in Rickford 1987: 27).

Rickford (1987) believes that even though the linguistic variation in such communities may be too complex to be represented by the single linear model, it can be covered by 'two or more simultaneously applicable unidimensional continua'. Carrington (1992: 97), however, believes that the unidimensional model is inherently flawed as an illustrative image: it encourages 'an interpretation of directionality, regardless of whether that is intended or not' and 'with the best will in the world, it is difficult to view [it] … as anything else than unidimensional'. Furthermore, any attempt to build on it, through the addition of other linear axes, does not increase its effectiveness, since it is simply not suited to the complexity of the phenomenon it seeks to describe. According to Carrington (1992: 98), linguists need to accept that 'creole space is multidimensional' and that the individuals in creole-speaking communities have 'multi-systemic repetoires'. Once this occurs, a more appropriate image can be found. He himself suggests the image of a marble cake, which 'allows the kind of blend and swirls that could depict the variable penetration of the upper, middle and lower layers into their neighbours … and does not imply obligatory directionality'. An alternative might be 'an integrated mass of soap bubbles, each of which has the unusual feature of a penetrable skin … [which] allows clusters of bubbles to penetrate one another without bursting'. The bubbles would have different shapes, and would elongate 'in whatever direction the wind blows … the overall shape of the mass would be arbitrary and irregular'. Though viable, the use of the multidimensional images has not been pursued in any great detail. It remains to be seen whether suggestions such as Carrington's will be developed by creolists investigating variation, or whether the unidimensional continuum (with or without modifications) will be retained for its seeming 'simplicity and versatility' (Carrington 1992: 96).

3.3.3 *Pidgin to creole to post-creole continuum?*

As we saw in Section 3.1, DeCamp assumed that the creole continuum emerged after social conditions in ex-colonial countries changed to allow varying degrees of access to a standard target. Alleyne (1971, 1980), however, suggests an alternative hypothesis: that continua in such societies existed from the earliest days of European–African co-existence, given that different slave groups had varying amounts of contact with their masters. For example, field slaves would have had the least amount of contact with their master and hence with the superstratal language, thus producing basilectal forms. House slaves, on the other hand, would have had the most prolonged and relatively intimate, daily contact with superstratal speakers and so would have produced acrolectal forms. Mesolectal forms would have been produced from groups in between the two, such as factory slaves. There does in fact seem to be some textual evidence for this: Rickford (1987: 33) states that two nineteenth-century pre-Emancipation sources (Bolingbroke 1807 and Claire 1834) contain contemporary examples of both basilectal and mesolectal usage among the slave and free Black populations in the Caribbean. In Alleyne's (1980: 194) view, there was initially little movement on the continuum since 'there was no pressure or motivation to adopt speech behaviours typical of other groups' but the social consequences of Emancipation resulted in 'the general adoption by each sector of the population of some of the speech characteristics of the social group above it'. Thus, Alleyne allows for post-Emancipation *decreolization*, or the increasing adoption of standard features, as does DeCamp; but where the latter sees it as the mechanism that creates the continuum, Alleyne views it as the one that causes speakers to move across it; passing from already extant basilectal and lower mesolectal varieties to higher mesolectal and acrolectal ones. Of course, restrictions which hamper a wholesale movement must apply, otherwise basilectal and mesolectal speakers would quickly disappear as everyone became acrolectal!

It is of course very difficult to prove that the continuum is a diachronic rather than a synchronic phenomenon, given the limitations that apply to twentieth-century hindsight. The history of, and actual usages present in, communities which today have 'continuum variation' was infrequently documented, making it practically impossible to make any kind of valid generalization about how long such varieties may have been in existence. At any rate, the question of whether the continuum is a pre- or post-Emancipation phenomenon has very little impact on how it is constructed (it is still represented in this view by the linear, unidimensional model) and on the linguistic analysis of its varieties.

In both synchronic (DeCamp) and diachronic (Alleyne) views of the continuum, one assumption has remained implicit: that speakers are primarily motivated to move towards the acrolect. This brings us to question (5).

3.3.4 Decreolization or recreolization?

It has been suggested that the nature of the linear, unidimensional continuum reflects and reinforces a view of the standard as 'positive' and the creole as 'negative'. Its linear representation forces us to read a movement from left (basilect) to right (acrolect), and suggests that this is the only possible movement: the 'obligatory directionality' referred to by Carrington (1992; see page 85). DeCamp's implicational scaling gives standard features a [+] sign and creole features [–], a usage that many of my own students have focused on as reflecting an underlying bias. Many of them have agreed with Haynes' (1973: 1; cited in Rickford 1987: 35) criticism that the continuum is an 'abstract construct which places people in the Caribbean on their hillsides, rolling the stones of phonological, syntactic and lexical mastery to a European summit, getting there, but never quite'. It is important to remember, though, that the model was based on a very real phenomenon that still exists. In the Anglophone Caribbean for instance, there is still considerable pressure to acquire standard English, the language of education, law, government and most of the media. Furthermore, it carries prestige and many individuals *want* to acquire it. Therefore, in areas such as Jamaica, where a creole is the mother tongue of most of the population but standard English the institutionalized language of 'progress', the continuum *would* inevitably evolve through the acquisition ([+]) of standard features as certain speakers moved towards the acrolect. It may seem an obvious thing to say, but the model essentially reflects the (to an extent, justified) assumption on which it was based.

Nevertheless, subsequent studies have revealed that movement across the continuum is more complex – the prestige of the standard is not the only powerful factor that operates in alleged continuum societies:

> One finds creole varieties proudly embraced as a symbol of local identity or national unity, or both (Le Page 1978); as a marker of working class membership and opposition to the dominant social order (Rickford 1983a); as an expression of one's preference for rural over urban life styles and values (W. Edwards 1973); and as an indicator of peer solidarity or informal style (Escure 1984a).
>
> (Rickford 1987: 36)

This covers cases of *recreolization*, a process often found, for example, among adolescents in these communities, who express peer group solidarity and resistance to authoritative structures by increased use of creole (often basilectal) forms. The same phenomenon can also be found, for example, in certain areas of London where youngsters, not always with a Caribbean (and specifically Jamaican) ethnic heritage, choose, over any other linguistic resource they might also possess, to use what has come to be known as London Jamaican (a fusion of their local London English and basilectal Anglophone creole forms) as a marker of peer group identity and of alienation from the dominant culture (see Sebba 1997: 225–33 for a more detailed discussion).

Thus speakers in 'post-creole speech communities', such as those of the Anglophone Caribbean are, like speakers everywhere, 'pulled' in different directions, according to their desire and ability to identify with various norms (see Chapter 1, Section 1.3.1): 'Caribbean speakers engage in style-shifting both up and down the continuum in everyday life, and although some people may be trying to increase their mastery or use of creole varieties, others are trying to do the same with SE [standard English]' (Rickford 1987: 36).[2] We are therefore brought back to the suggestion that the model as it stands may not be appropriate, since it does not reflect speakers' multi-systemic repertoires nor the fact that movement across the continuum is not unidirectional (Carrington 1992; see page 85 of this volume). As stated above, it seems that there is still much to be done in the area of (re)shaping a new, more representative, image.

Despite the many criticisms that have been levelled at it, the creole continuum model still remains a cornerstone of creole studies, perhaps because it was the first real attempt to describe as simply and as effectively as possible a *particular* type of variation that emerges from a *particular* type of language contact. Accordingly, its usefulness has been demonstrated outside of creolistics: O'Donnell and Todd (1980: 53), for example, apply it to a description of the variation that may occur in the speech of northern Irish, Catholic, native Gaelic speakers who also have varying degrees of proficiency in English. As far as creole studies is concerned, however, it has helped the field 'gain some very solid ground (as well as some rather boggy terrain) so that many of the aspects of dealing with decreolizing varieties are much less daunting today than they were 20 years ago' (Holm 1988: 59).

Endnotes

1. Even though this is true of both extended pidgins and creoles, I shall be dealing only with the latter in this chapter, since the continuum model was devised on the basis of data from creole-using communities.
2. This can be viewed in terms of the Labovian (1972) idea of *overt* and *covert prestige*, which seems to apply in many speech communities: some

speakers move towards acquiring forms that have high social status, or overt prestige (such as standard English); while others are drawn towards forms which have covert prestige, or little or no social standing, but embody certain values or perspectives that are important to that group, as in the case of young London Jamaican users.

|4|

Crick crack, monkey break 'e back for a piece of pommerac Language planning

4.1 Introduction

Now that we have examined issues which pertain to the pidgin and creole past (for example, questions of genesis) and to the present (such as variation, encoded in the creole continuum), it seems appropriate to round off with looking to their future: in a world that is increasingly shrinking, through the globalization of languages such as English, is there room for such languages?

Such questions have been the focus for creolists interested in the area of language planning. In the following sections we shall explore some of the issues in more detail using examples from creole-speaking communities in the Atlantic and Pacific region. First, however, we shall turn our attention to language planning: what does it mean, and what does it involve?

4.2 Language planning: definitions and stages

Put quite simply, language planning often takes place in multilingual (and sometimes multidialectal) societies and involves the making of decisions as to what language (or what variety of language) will serve what function. As Fasold (1984: 246) points out, the term 'planning' implies that the choices made in this respect will be deliberate and explicit. They will also be made by those who wield power in the society, and therefore have the authority to have those decisions implemented.

One famous example of language planning can be seen in the establishment of the Académie Française in the seventeenth century, on the invitation of the influential and powerful Cardinal Richelieu. The Académie had its roots in a small contingent intially brought together by Valentin Conart, a rich and ardent collector of books and a lover of literature. Conart was also a member of the Hôtel de Rambouillet, an elite club of aristocrats and popular contemporary authors, who frequently met to read and discuss the latest literary offerings and also to debate questions of linguistic usage; a concern that had begun in the sixteenth century. The Renaissance had resulted in a renewed and enthusiastic interest in reading and emulating the works of classical (Latin) scholars but this, paradoxically, occurred at a time when the vernacular languages of Europe were coming into their own and displacing Latin as the established language of scholarship and erudition. In France, this meant that a standardized and literary French began to take shape; a French that was 'purified', stable and fit to serve as the language of theology, academia, literature, government and any other prestigious domain. And it was those educated in the classical tradition, such as the members of the Hôtel, who endlessly debated the purification of French. By about 1629, a small number of scholars interested in language and literature began to meet at Conart's house, 'an atmosphere free of the condescension they felt at the Hôtel de Rambouillet' (Cooper 1989: 9). Richelieu, finding the existence of 'a cultural center that was independent of his control … intolerable' (Maland 1970: 96; quoted in Cooper 1989: 10), proposed that they form an official body that would be guaranteed state support. The members reluctantly accepted the Cardinal's 'invitation' and met for the first time on 13 March 1634 as the Académie Française.

One of Richelieu's main aims in establishing this body was to achieve regulation of the emerging standard: he wanted the Académie to undertake the work of purification; cleansing it of all that was coarse, vulgar, unnecessary (all prescriptive and inevitably socially biased judgements) and turning it into 'an imperial language', one of 'high culture and power' (Cooper 1989: 10). Thus, the Académie's main function was 'to give explicit rules to our language and to render it pure, eloquent and capable of treating the arts and sciences' (quoted in 1989: 10). It was therefore to undertake *corpus planning* (a term used in language planning to refer to the defining and explication of rules for linguistic usage, primarily in the written medium). To this end, the Académie was charged with producing regulatory works: a treatise on rhetoric and poetic usage, a grammar and a dictionary (the latter of which would also standardize ortho-graphical conventions).[1] Once it was evident that French could exist in a 'pure', regulated and eminently usable state, awareness of its 'worthwhile' nature (vis-à-vis Latin) would grow. It is noteworthy, though, that *status planning*, or raising the social profile of the chosen variety, often takes place through governmental policies that officially sanction its use in public institutions such as those of law, education and the media.

Scholars of eighteenth-century England such as Jonathan Swift believed that the development of English, as the language of a grow-ing colonial power, should be modelled on the French example. Indeed, Swift proposed that an English Academy should also be established, whose main aim (like that of its French cousin) would be to regulate on the development and usage of standard English:

> I do here in the name of all the learned and polite persons of the nation complain ... that our language [that is, English] is extremely imperfect. .... In order to reform our language, I con-ceive ... that a free judicious choice should be made of such per-sons, as are generally allowed to be best qualified for such a work. ... These, to a certain number at least, should assemble at some appointed time and place, and *fix on rules*, by which they design to proceed. .... The persons who are to undertake this work will have the example of the French before them to imitate, where they have proceeded right, and to avoid their mistakes.
>
> (Swift 1712; in Baugh and Cable 1978: 265; emphasis mine)

Though a formal English Academy never materialized, corpus plan-ning of the emerging standard was nevertheless undertaken by lexi-cographers (that is, dictionary-makers) such as Samuel Johnson and prescriptive grammarians such as Robert Lowth. The work of such scholars (and the public demand for it) aided in status planning: stan-dard English, as the codified variety of the educated, was elevated to the socially prestigious position it still enjoys today.

As stated on page 90, language planning also takes place in communities where more than one language exists. One such exam-ple can be seen in the promotion of Hebrew in Palestine. In the mid-nineteenth century, Jewish migration into Palestine (a land Jews view as their ancestral home) was steadily increasing. They comprised, however, different communities, each with its own language: Jews from eastern Europe spoke Yiddish; those from countries part of the once powerful Ottoman Empire, Judezmo or Arabic; and those from North Africa and western Asia, Arabic. Nevertheless, the one language of which a large part of the male population had varying degrees of knowledge was Hebrew. The latter had ceased to be an everyday vernacular around AD 200 but had continued to be used in the written medium, as a language of prayer, theology and even of law, science and philosophy. Thus, many educated, male nineteenth-century Jews, like their forefathers, could read and write Hebrew. In addition, it was also occasionally used in the spoken medium as a lingua franca, albeit in restricted contexts, such as in the marketplace. Thus, when the call for a common Jewish language came, Hebrew seemed the natural choice.

The revival of this language as an everyday medium of communication had its roots in the European nationalist movements of the 1880s. Language, more specifically linguistic identity, played a key role in these:

> Language served these movements as a symbol around which proto-elites could create a nationalist self-consciousness and a respectable focus for nationalist aspirations. ... A common language symbolized the unity of those who spoke it ... expressed their uniqueness, highlighted the difference between them and those who ruled them via an alien tongue, and legitimized their self-assertion and their struggle for autonomy.

> (Cooper 1989: 12)

Eliezer Ben Yehuda, a Russian Jew who arrived in Palestine in 1881, spearheaded the movement for promoting Hebrew and proposed that it be the official medium of instruction in the schools of Jewish settlements. Kindergartens (from 1898) and high schools (from 1906) where Hebrew was the sole language used were established, and in the early years of the twentieth century:

> young couples began to enter into matrimony who had gone through the Hebrew school and whose Hebrew speech was fluent and natural. At that time were born the first children in families who spoke nothing but Hebrew in the home, and those babies grew up in Hebrew without anyone making a special effort to assure this. They were the first people, after a lapse of 1,700 years, who knew no language but Hebrew.

> (Rabin 1973: 73; quoted in Cooper 1989: 13)

One of the very interesting things about the Hebrew revival was that corpus and status planning had to be geared not towards making Hebrew linguistically 'fit' and socially prestigious (as in the case of standard French and standard English) but, instead, towards 'vernacularizing' it – that is, equipping it with the resources to function as a language of everyday activities. Nevertheless, the idealism, enthusiasm and nationalist aspirations of Jewish immigrants ensured that this occurred successfully and in so doing, helped to lay 'the foundations of the modern Israeli state' (Cooper 1989: 14).

As we can see from the above examples, language planning often takes place as part of wider socio-political issues and, as such, is motivated by a particular ideology. Cobarrubias and Fishman (1983: 63–6) identified four such precepts (outlined below) which underlie language planning strategies.

LINGUISTIC PLURALISM

Language planning strategies with this aim in mind support the 'co-existence of different language groups and their right to maintain and cultivate their languages on an equitable basis' (Cobarrubias and Fishman 1983: 65). This has been the case in Belgium, for example, where French is the official language of the south, Flemish of the north and German of the east. French and Flemish are both officially recognized in Brussels.

LINGUISTIC ASSIMILATION AND PURISM

Strategies with linguistic assimilation as their goal seek to ensure (in theory) that all members of a speech community have the ability to use the dominant language. In such cases, the rights of linguistic minorities are often ignored. In 1938, for example, the government of the former Soviet Union stipulated that all non-Russian schools had to teach Russian as a second language. Even though schools were later granted the right to choose their language of education in 1958, Russian essentially retained domination in the schoolroom, so much so that pupils in most Russian Republics received their primary and secondary schooling in this language, with little or no concession made to their respective mother tongues (Daoust 1997: 442).

Cobarrubias and Fishman (1983: 65) define linguistic purism as a close relation of linguistic assimilation, since it is shaped by the same principles and achieves similar results. With linguistic purism, an 'ideal' form of a language, which exists primarily in the written medium and is therefore somewhat estranged from the variation that characterizes everyday speech, is promoted. 'This form of language is associated with specific aesthetic and sometimes moral values which represent the speech community's social ideal and norm' (Labov 1972). The idea that to become fully competent in the use of this form guarantees social recognition and progress (in other words, the establishment of a linguistic meritocracy where attributes such as ethnicity and gender are neutralized!) is also fostered and advanced by institutions such as the education system and, in some cases, by language academies. Thus, non-'ideal' forms of that language come to be seen as deviant, and their use in domains where the 'ideal' form dominates is discouraged or repressed. Indeed, the search for linguistic purism motivated our first two examples of language planning. As stated on page 91, the French Académie was set up to regulate the development of standard French, a variety that existed (as standards tend to do) mainly in the written form. The post-Revolution government of eighteenth-century France decreed that this standard (partly codified by a dictionary of usage) was to be the sole language of primary schools, and also of the law. In addition, the orthographic conventions devised by the Académie Française were made compulsory in 1832. In passing such laws, the government hoped not only to make knowledge of standard conventions as widespread as possible, but also to wipe out use of what it believed to be 'impure' varieties of French.

Closer to home, the drive to promote standard English (again existing primarily in the written medium) has been ongoing since the eighteenth century. Though, as stated above, an English Academy was never established, competence in standard English is still considered an important social asset, whereas that in non-standard varieties is often trivialized or characterized as an inability to use 'proper English'. Standard English is also associated for some with high moral and aesthetic values, as can be seen in John Rae's (1982) statement that one of the most important arguments for teaching it is that 'attention to the rules of grammar and care in the choice of words encourages punctiliousness in other matters ... such as honesty, responsibility, propriety, gratitude [and] apology'. Because its use is so widespread, as a medium for textbooks, newspapers, essay writing, government and legal documents, and so on, we have come to see it as a norm: many believe that it is the *only* English that can be used for such purposes. Indeed, many believe that it is the *only* 'correct' form of English.

VERNACULARIZATION

Language planning decisions that aim for vernacularization have indigenous languages or those which are widely known in a community, officially recognized instead of, or alongside, an international language of wider communication. In Haiti, for example, the indigenous French-lexifier creole has official status along with French. Similarly, Bislama (the Melanesian Pidgin English spoken in Vanuatu; see Chapter 2), is one of the island's three official languages; the other two being English and French. The restoration and adoption of Hebrew, a literary and liturgical language, as an everyday means of communication among Palestinian Jews (discussed earlier) is also an example of vernacularization.

INTERNATIONALISM

When internationalism becomes an aim for language planners, what usually results is the adoption, or maintenance, of a language of wider communication in an official capacity. It is believed that this decision will allow for socio-economic participation on an international level. However, the promotion of this international language often entails the marginalization of indigenous languages and their speakers, since it is typically a socially powerful elite minority who are competent in the use of the international language. Their 'hold' on the language not only invests it with prestige but also maintains their socio-political power.

Internationalism has been the goal of the language planning policies of quite a few creole-speaking territories, such as those of the Anglophone Caribbean. Trinidad, as we shall see in the following section, is one such area; and the discussion of the policies of language use in this island can be extended to others such as Barbados, Guyana, Antigua and Jamaica, where English-lexifier creoles are the mother tongues of the majority of each population.

4.3 Case study: language planning in Trinidad

Arends *et al.* (1995: 65) state that 'since the end of the Second World War, a world wide process of decolonization has taken place'. Many territories that had been held and governed by various European nations for centuries began to question this ownership, feeding the call for political and cultural autonomy from the colonizer. This was the case in Trinidad, a Caribbean island (of the Republic of Trinidad and Tobago) that had been claimed by the Spanish in 1498, settled by the French (under treaty with Spain) from 1763, seized by the British in 1797 and officially ceded to them in 1802. Britain held the island until 1962 when it was granted independence.[2]

Trinidad, like many other ex-colonies, has retained certain political ties with Britain which had, after all, established much of the nation's infrastructure when the territory was gained in the nineteenth century. Thus, the education system was based on the British model, with grammar schools and Common Entrance examinations (still in use for all pupils). Students did O-level (now replaced by papers set by the Caribbean Examinations Council (CXC)) and still do A-level examinations (adjudicated by Cambridge University). The legal system is also based on English law, and the highest court of appeal, at the time of writing, is the English Privy Council. The language of such institutions is (British standard) English, a decision that had been made in 1823, when it was given official status.

The island is, however, home to other languages. As indicated in Chapters 2 and 3, a French-based creole (TFC), one reminder of the nation's Gallic past, is still used by a dwindling minority. In the nineteenth century, 145 000 East Indians were imported into the island as indentured labour. The majority spoke Bhojpuri, which remained the first language of many with East Indian ethnicity until approximately the 1930s. In this century, the island has also become home to a small Chinese population, some of whom have retained their native language in private domains, as do a settled Lebanese community. For the majority of those born on the island, however, an English-lexifier creole (TEC) has served as a mother tongue. This creole was formed in the early years of British settlement and fostered by mass influxes of speakers of other English-lexifier creoles from British territories, such as Barbados, in the nineteenth century. It has also been a second, or third, language for some. For example, younger generations in the French-lexifier creole-speaking community of Paramín have increasingly become (through growing interaction with the wider community) bilingual in TEC. Many East Indians of my grandparents' generation (born in the first 20 years of this century) spoke Bhojpuri natively, the French-lexifier creole (which they encountered in rural settlements) as a second language and eventually, as their contact with such speakers grew, TEC. Such multilingualism has nurtured the transference of many TFC and Bhojpuri lexical items and phrases into the English-lexifier creole: TEC has **calques** such as *it eating good* (French/TFC *il mange bien*); *it making cold* (French/TFC *il fait froid*); expressions such as *toute bagaille* 'bag and baggage', *maljo* 'bad/evil

eye' from French/TFC *mal yeux*, *mauvais langue* 'bad mouth; speaking ill of someone', *tantie* 'aunt' from French/TFC *tante* and *zaboca*
'avocado(es)' from French/TFC *les avocats*.[3] East Indian food and
kinship terms have become firmly entrenched in TEC: all speakers,
regardless of ethnicity, will recognize and use *dulaha* and *dulahin*
'bridegroom' and 'bride' respectively, *nana* and *nani* (maternal grandfather and grandmother), *khaka* and *khaki* (paternal grandfather and
grandmother). The nation's favourite food is *roti*, an unleavened bread
which can have a variety of fillings, such as curried *channa* 'chickpeas'
and *alloo* 'potatoes', or *bhaji* 'spinach'.[4] Despite such additions, however, the relationship between the creole and its superstratal parent,
English, remains explicit. As we shall see, this has in fact been to the
creole's disadvantage in language planning strategies.

When islands such as Martinique, Guadeloupe and Guyane
asserted their independence from France, the status of their French-
lexifier creoles became an important issue in the anti-colonial movement (cf. Cooper 1989: 12; quoted on page 93). Similar levels of
consideration, however, were not accorded English-lexifier creoles in
the drive for independence in British-held territories. In these areas,

> the few who displayed any form of language consciousness at all,
> viewed Creole [*sic*] as simply another of the unfortunate by-prod-
> ucts of colonialism. According to this position, the use of 'bro-
> ken forms of English', i.e. English-lexicon Creole languages,
> would cease in the post-colonial period as a result of the expo-
> sure of the mass of the population to 'proper English'. This was
> to be achieved by way of an improved education system, increased
> access to written material and information in English etc.
>
> (Devonish 1986: 88)

This has certainly been the case in Trinidad, where TEC has been,
and still is, variously referred to as 'bad/broken English', 'slang' or
'dialect'; the latter term indicating that it does not, for many native
speakers, have the status of a full language. Such denigration is not
reserved only for English-lexifier creoles – indeed, many are labelled
derogatorily. On the whole, creoles 'have acquired negative values
arising from their associations with slavery and degradation' (Winer
1990: 239). In addition, they have historically been ridiculed and
marginalized by European travellers and colonizers (see Chapter 1).
Thus native speakers contextualize these languages against a background of powerlessness, oppression and ridicule – a 'shameful'

legacy. For many, to continue to use (and in so doing, validate) creoles is to constantly reinforce the colonial yoke.

The situation is worsened further for creoles like TEC in that the influence of the superstratal parent in its formation and subsequent development has been so great that many native speakers erroneously assume that it is not a separate language but English learned imperfectly; an idea that has been applied to other creoles with a similar history, such as the English-lexifier creole of Barbados. Consequently, there is a long-established tradition of dismissing TEC as a shameful (or laughable, depending on the perspective) distortion of the 'norm' of standard English. For example, nineteenth-century newspapers, such as the *Trinidad Spectator*, would amuse their readers with fictionalized accounts of the 'adventures' of TEC native speakers, who were invariably Black, poor and uneducated (thus reinforcing the links between 'bad English', marked ethnicity, low social class and powerlessness). The TEC speakers would be portrayed through their native creole 'voice', but were often prefaced, and so contextualized, by one that adopted standard English. Many explicitly condemned or ridiculed TEC (and, by extension, its speakers), as in the following prefatory letters (full texts given in Appendix).[5]

(a) Mr Editor – I calculate that the last palaver [a conversation in TEC] I sent you, was pretty considerably amusing to some of your folk; I take the liberty of sending you a little more of the same kind of gibberish, which you may use or abuse, as you think proper.

> I am,
> Jerry

[text in TEC follows]

(*Trinidad Spectator*; 8 November 1845)

(b) Standing at my window one Sunday morning, I overheard a conversation between two of my Negroes which was so interesting – larded with their quaint idioms and humourous (*sic*) proverbs, expressed in those most ludicrous dialects, negro English and creole French, that I with difficulty refrained from laughter. ...

> Yours, &c.
> Matthew Muscovado

[TEC text follows]

(*Trinidad Guardian*; 2 October 1827)

The same attitude was manifested in other institutions, such as the legal and education systems. The following extract is from the *Trinidad Guardian*'s 'From our Files' column, which reprints articles first run at least two decades previously. The article refers to the use of *Patois*, which is the local term for the French-lexifier creole, but the sentiments would very likely have been the same if the issue had been about TEC: despite the fact that English is the official language of the law, some defendants and witnesses do not use it. The underlying assumption, expressed by both the writer and the quoted Royal Magistrate, is that these speakers indeed have a competent grasp of (standard) English but perversely and deliberately avoid it:

FROM OUR FILES

75 YEARS AGO

Evidence in Patois

WHILE English is the official language of the local law courts, yet it not unfrequently happens, writes a correspondent, that evidence is given there in a foreign language, thereby necessitating the services of an interpreter. It is quite true that a person should use the language he can speak well, *but is it right for him to give evidence in a foreign language when he can do the same in English?...*

It has been said that residents of Maraval and Diego Martin prefer to give evidence in Patois rather than English for fear of getting muddled during cross-examination. *The Hon RM Lazare has given it as his opinion that they do this because they have a kind of superstition that Patois expresses their thoughts more correctly.*

(*Trinidad Guardian* 7 July 1997: 27; emphasis mine)

The same column had, about a month earlier, re-run an article first published in 1937. This time, the focus was on attempts to encourage literacy in standard English in schools, which ranged from instructing teachers on how to stamp out creole in the classroom to rewarding written competence in the official language:

FROM OUR FILES

60 YEARS AGO

Courses for teachers

THERE IS now in preparation a course of lectures in the teaching of English to be delivered to teachers of the colony by C. Farrell, BA, assistant master of Queen's Royal College, *who has been conducting experiments with the boys of the college to get rid of the use of 'creolisms'*.

This announcement was made by the Hon'ble [*sic*] Captain J.O. Cutteridge, MBE, the Director of Education, on Friday afternoon last when he made the presentation of the Green Pastures (Junior) Shield, won by the Arouca Government School of which E.W. Henry is the headteacher.

This was the first occasion in which this school has won the shield which was offered as a first prize for the best essay submitted, and for which no fewer than 175 schools in Trinidad and Tobago and Grenada competed.

(*Trinidad Guardian* 14 June 1997: 31; emphasis mine)

Aversion to forms other than British standard English, then, was the prevailing attitude when the colony achieved independence in 1962. However, the anti-colonial movement also brought to the forefront those few who viewed creoles not as an embarrassment but as important symbols of national identity. Proponents of folk culture such as Paul Keens Douglas (much like Louise Bennett of Jamaica and Wordsworth McAndrew of Guyana) and authors such as Samuel Selvon expressed their allegiance to TEC by performing and writing in it, as well as 'researching and popularising many aspects of the local culture, notably folk tales and folk songs' (Devonish 1986: 88). Trinidad, like many other islands, also had (and continues to have) a thriving calypso tradition. The lyrics of these songs, which often offer topical commentary but which have also increasingly moved into the realm of local dance music, have always been in TEC. Though existing primarily in the oral medium, many came to be written down for popular and scholarly reference, thus reinforcing the folklorist tradition referred to above.

However, Devonish (1986) also states that while their work was invaluable in raising awareness of creoles as effective and positive identity markers, certain artistic 'crusaders' still believed in the absolute authority of standard English:

they ended up stressing the need for the *preservation* [sic] of
Creole in its existing roles and functions ... in spite of the
expressiveness and efficiency of Creole as a medium of communication, the role of English as the sole official language could
not be challenged.

This may certainly have been true for Trinidadian authors such as the
Naipauls and de Boissière, who broke with the tradition of using creole for denigratory and/or humorous purposes (see page 99), and created instead real and immediate characters for whom TEC was
simply the everyday language of life. However, their stories unfolded
through a standard English omniscient narrator, the dominant voice,
as can be seen in the following excerpt from *Crown Jewel*:

> 'They takin away me things and I haven't a cent. You could lend
> me four dollars till the end of month, Miss Aurelia?' The timid-
> ity in her husky voice indicated that this was a last desperate
> effort to raise the four dollars, that she was uncertain whether
> to give way to fear, grief or rage.
>
> (de Boissière 1952: 118)

Thus in Trinidad, as in other ex-British colonies, such artists
helped to raise the profile of the creole but only to certain limits: its
use in certain domains, such as in performances and literature meant
for a local audience, became acceptable and a symbol of *local* identity, but not much more.

None the less, after 1962, TEC slowly began to seep into other
areas from which it had previously been excluded. In the political
arena, for example, TEC has come to be used in speeches seeking to
establish the speaker as 'for and with the people'. It is therefore used
for sloganeering, jokes and as an 'emotional rhetorical device'
(Devonish 1986: 100). However, since English has remained the official language of government and administration, such TEC usage is
again firmly embedded in standard English narrative. The media,
too, largely conform to official language policy: standard English is
the main vehicle of commentary and reporting. However, TEC is
now often used for specific purposes. In newspapers, writers of
'entertainment' columns will use TEC. Paul Keens-Douglas, for
example, wrote a lighthearted column called *Is Town Say So*
(*Trinidad Express* 1984), which expressed the views of the ordinary
citizen (often without a real voice in media reporting) on a range of

topical issues. As can be seen in the following extract, the omniscient narrator also has a creole voice:

> De moment Veda hear dat de Prime Minister goin' on tour quite up in Matura, Veda *get vex*. Now Veda livin' in Woodbrook, an' dat is wha' cause de whole problem. She say, 'How de hell de Prime Minister goin' on tour *quite up in Matura* an' he eh even *make ah lil pass by Woodbrook?*'

> (Keens-Douglas 1984: 16)

TEC (vs BRITISH STANDARD ENGLISH) FEATURES

- [d] for [ð], as in *de* 'the' and *dat* 'that'
- [n] for word final [ŋ], as in *livin'* and *goin'*
- use of *eh* (possibly derived from *ain't*) as a marker of negation
- no inflectional marking of the past tense, as in *hear* 'heard', *get* 'got'
- no form of auxiliary *to be* in progressive aspect constructions: *Veda livin' in Woodbrook* 'Veda is living in Woodbrook'
- *get vex*: 'got/became annoyed'
- *quite up in Matura*: 'all the way to Matura'
- *make ah lil pass by Woodbrook*: 'come for a quick visit to Woodbrook'

Cartoonists commenting on local topical issues and/or portraying local characters will also use TEC (see Figures 4.1 and 4.2).

Source: Trinidad Express 3 June 1999

Figure 4.1 *Patrick, if dis eh work ...*

Source: *Trinidad Express* 18 July 1999

Figure 4.2   Sweetbread

TEC (vs BRITISH STANDARD ENGLISH) FEATURES
(in addition to [d] for [ð] and the use of *eh*; see Keens-Douglas
(1984: 16)):

Cartoon (a)
- *crapaud smoke yuh pipe*: 'you're all washed up'

Cartoon (b)
- use of adjectives as verbs (see Chapter 2) in phrases where
  standard English would use a copula; as in *some people
  stingy, when yuh rich and stingy, dat real bad* and *she poor*

In the reporting of news events, TEC quotes from persons interviewed will be included verbatim, as in the following excerpt from a
piece about a local gathering's failure to recognize Wendy Fitzwilliam
(winner of the Miss Universe pageant in 1999) at a popular pub:

> Those who did recognise her actually doubted themselves, justi-
> fying their conclusions with the argument that the queen would
> never be allowed to walk among lowly commoners without a
> battery of officious security guards. Some of them actually
> scoffed at the gall of this young woman who, they said, 'feel dat
> we doh know we Wendy'.

(Trinidad Express 9 May 1999)

Advertisements in newspapers and on television and radio will sometimes use the creole in their strap lines or slogans, as can be seen in

Figure 4.3, a promotion for Barbados' harvest festival (*Crop Over*) in the *Trinidad Guardian*.

Figure 4.3 'Barbados Crop Over Festival is here again . . .'

Source: Trinidad Guardian 24 July 1999

TEC FEATURES

- *More than a Carnival – <u>Sweet Fuh Days</u>*: Trinidad's Carnival officially takes place on the Monday and Tuesday preceding Ash Wednesday. This advertisement states that the festival in Barbados promises a good time (that is, is *sweet*) for a longer period. Hence *sweet fuh days* (*fuh* denoting the casual/basilectal pronunciation [fə]; see chapter 3) means 'a good time for a long time!'.
- *The tents are on and Calypso <u>'can' done</u> . . .*: 'the musical entertainment [*tents*, in which it takes place] is on, and you won't be able to <u>get enough of</u> the calypso' (*'can' done = can't done*).

Despite such breakthroughs, the use of TEC in the media (even of highly acrolectal versions, as seen in Chapter 3), vis-à-vis that of standard English, essentially remains limited.

An area in which language policy is often made explicit is that of education, though Devonish (1986: 119) states that this is rather like putting the proverbial cart before the horse: to implement language policy in the schools without attempting 'a more general reform in the roles and functions of the various languages used in society as a whole' is 'a recipe for confusion, non-cooperation and resistance to language education measures by parents and teachers alike'. As a consequence, such policies become ineffective, since the schools continue to 'reproduce and reinforce [social] norms', including those of 'language use and language acceptability' (Devonish 1986: 101). As indicated in the article quoted on page 101, Trinidad, like its Caribbean Commonwealth counterparts, inherited an education system whose official language policy was that British standard English was the sole medium of instruction as well as the language in which literacy was to be acquired. Devonish (1986) states that 'the assumption underlying this language education policy was that those who entered the education system were, in fact, native speakers of English, English-lexicon Creole [*sic*] being no more than a form of "broken English" which had to be corrected by the education system' (cf. *Courses for Teachers*, page 101); a notion that schools inevitably perpetuated.

This assumption, however, was severely challenged in the post-independence period which, in ushering in an era of increasing accessibility to public education, saw a massive influx of native TEC speakers with little or no competence in standard English into the school system. Poor academic performance, as well as high failure rates in English (Craig (1971: 376) quotes a 60–85 per cent failure rate at all levels of English learning in most Caribbean Commonwealth territories) were inevitable results; inevitable since the educators had missed a crucial point. In making English the sole language of instruction, they were placing a tremendous burden on native TEC-speaking children: the latter were not only dealing with the demands of the curriculum, they were essentially doing it in a foreign language. Furthermore, the fact that their native language was either being ignored or devalued as 'bad English' very likely resulted in a measure of psychological humiliation, eroding their motivation to learn.[6] To adapt Coard (1971; quoted in Winer 1990: 240), to communicate the idea that someone's native culture and language is second rate, is to accuse *them* of *being* second rate.

Winer (1990: 245) states that in 1975 the Trinidad Ministry of Education, in seeking to ameliorate this situation, amended official language education policy: it formally recognized TEC as the native language of the majority of schoolchildren and one which could be used in both oral and written media. The syllabus advocated the use of 'teaching strategies based on the differences between the two' (i.e. TEC and British standard English) (1990: 245) and stated that TEC could and should be incorporated into schoolwork and examinations. In encouraging the use of TEC in the classroom, the Ministry of Education was adopting a policy of *transitional bilingualism* (Craig 1980: 250–2).[7] The belief was that if the school recognized TEC as a *language* which was distinct from English, students would no longer feel disenfranchised by an alien system, would begin to engage with the curriculum and, instead of 'jumping in at the deep end', would smoothly and gradually move into acquiring literacy skills in standard English, as they would with any other foreign language.

Despite the fact that the ultimate aim was achieving competence in standard English, these recommendations were not generally welcomed. Both parents and teachers alike, no doubt still holding on to the belief that the creole was 'bad/broken English', were concerned that the school's acknowledgement and use of TEC would not only inhibit the learning of 'proper English', but would also lead students to the erroneous conclusion that the creole was appropriate in formal domains. This belief would severely limit 'opportunities for successful education and employment' (Winer 1990: 245).

Winer, writing in 1990, stated that this was no longer the prevailing attitude in Trinidad and the rest of the Commonwealth Caribbean. There had instead been 'increased acceptance of 'dialect' in schools, including writing of songs, poems, plays and stories (especially dialogue) in creole, and significantly, the opportunity to write in Creole on the O-Level English examinations set by the regional Caribbean Examinations Council' (Winer 1990: 241). I have to say, as a native Trinidadian who received all my primary, secondary and undergraduate education in the island roughly between 1973 and 1989, these are not the policies I remember. In primary school (1973–1979), we were subjected to corporal punishment for 'creolisms' in written and oral work in the classroom. The tradition of assuming that English was our native language went unchallenged. In secondary school, native-speaker competence in TEC was ignored, or penalized in written work by low grades. It was not until I started undergraduate work at the University of the West Indies, which ran (and still does) courses in pidgin and creole studies that I consciously realized the validity of TEC as a language. It is highly likely that Trinidadian schoolchildren like me suffered from a lack of *implementation* of the Ministry of Education directives. This is not at all an uncommon occurrence for language planners. Arends *et al.* (1995: 67) state that, often:

Although governmental institutions may be powerful, the language behaviour of individuals may conflict with the official policies. Personal attitudes turn out to be related to the social distribution of languages in the community, and the social meanings attached to these languages.

Thus, even though the use of TEC in schools had governmental sanction, at the level of school boards and PTAs, decisions may have been taken to continue using the traditional methods (of punishment and/or marginalization of the creole) to achieve literacy in standard English. Such resolutions would have been based on the 'personal attitudes' of parents and teachers, who would have had an awareness of the 'social meanings' and 'social distribution' of the languages in question: use of English, the language long associated in the colonies with civilization and progess, would have been seen as increasing the chances of social mobility, educational and employment opportunities; while use of TEC, the language born in the slave barracks, would have been seen as 'ghetto-izing' its speakers.

In 1993, the National Task Force for Education published the Education Policy Paper, which sets out Trinidad's educational objectives for the period 1993–2003. The Paper states that the basic goals are the achievement of literacy, numeracy, problem-solving and social competency skills. These should be acquired by children at the end of the primary cycle of education. It is clear that 'literacy' means literacy in standard English:

3.10.5 There should therefore be a language policy at the primary level and indeed at all levels which:
   (a) spells out minimum levels of competence to be attained in the official standard language;
   (b) provides guiding principles for teaching language across the curriculum;
   (c) sets out guidelines for effectively utilising the 'dialect' in maximising general educational development in such areas as early reading and literacy;
   (d) addresses the development of an explicit awareness of the pupil's intuitive knowledge of the 'dialect';
   (e) facilitates the introduction and/or development of other languages relevant to our socio-economic context.

Students at the end of the primary cycle should therefore be able to:

i. express themselves clearly and effectively through speech and writing by means of standard English;
ii. listen with a high degree of understanding to instructions, descriptions, explanations, narrations in standard English in a familiar accent and in the vocabulary and sentence structure appropriate to their age;
iii. read, with a high degree of understanding, instructions, descriptions, explanations, narrations in standard English in the vocabulary and sentence structure appropriate to their age;
iv. think creatively;
v. respond sensitively to varied and meaningful Literature and other forms of art at the appropriate level.

It would seem that the educators' hope is that the transition to becoming standard English users will have been achieved by the time students start secondary school. Accordingly, no such aims and goals are set out for secondary-level students: it is assumed that they will have acquired the 'skills for communication required for the changing world environment in adult life' (Education Policy Paper: 172).

The language situation in Trinidad can therefore be summed up as follows: TEC, the native language of the majority of the population, co-exists with British standard English, the official language of the country. TEC, like many other creoles, has had a long history of denigration but after independence in 1962, began to be used in limited ways in domains formerly the preserve of standard English. Education is the only area in which language policy has ever been officially stated. It is clearly one with *internationalism* as its goal, and it seeks to achieve it through a programme of transitional bilingualism. Is it likely to succeed?

4.3.1 Issues and problems in language planning

As stated in the previous section, the language situation outlined for Trinidad is not dissimilar to that found in many other creole-speaking territories. Problems of language planning in the island are also faced elsewhere. Since language planning policy has been explicit only in the area of education, it is here that the discussion will be concentrated.

Arends *et al.* (1995: 66) state that the main processes of language planning include:

a1 setting of goals;

a2 implementing of these goals;

a3 evaluating both the attainment of the original goals and methods of implementation. This may lead to the formulation of new goals, which is the starting point for a new cycle of language planning activities.

The problems that typically hinder the carrying out of these processes often have to do with:

b1 the nature of the remaining colonial ties

b2 the nature of linguistic diversity

b3 the developmental state of the indigenous languages

b4 the language attitude among the speakers

These are all points relevant to the Trinidad situation. Education policy has always had a definite goal (a1), namely the acquisition of literacy in British standard English. Initially, steps taken to implement this goal (a2) included maintaining standard English as the official medium of instruction in education and delivering an English-centric curriculum, using only standard English materials and texts. Later evaluation of goals and implementation (a3), in the light of high failure rates, caused a reassessment not of the original goal, but of the methods of implementation. Educators now advocate the use of TEC to facilitate acquisition of the official language. It is, however, at this stage in the process, that problems have arisen. A 'new cycle' of language planning activities has not begun. Why?

Two major reasons are stated in (b1) and (b4): the nature of the remaining colonial ties and language attitudes of speakers. Having gained independence only 37 years ago, Trinidad is still a 'young' country that is not yet fully confident in its 'freedom', largely because so much of the colonial legacy has remained in its infrastructure (see page 97). Thus, since Trinidadians continue to be educated and socialized in a system that sets up English language and culture as norms to be attained or at least striven for, they also continue to adopt the perspective that their creole simply does not come up to scratch. The old 'colonial mentality' therefore defines the language attitudes of many native Trinidadians. Winer (1993: 59) illustrates this with an excerpt from a letter written to the *Trinidad Express* (19 October 1986: 10):

to create a Trinidad dialect [to foster Trinidad's English-lexifier creole] is to butcher Oxford English – the English in which all

West Indian scholars excel. ... We are too lazy to pronounce and enunciate correctly. We want short cuts to everything.

We see here the expression of the English-centric view that the creole itself is linguistically inadequate, a 'butchery' of standard English. Note that such sentiments are not unlike those expressed by early European chroniclers of pidgins and creoles (see Chapter 1).

Practical considerations too affect language attitudes. Areas like Trinidad are not global powers; their economic success is dependent on the wider world, a large part of which is English-speaking. Individual success and mobility on an international level is also often reliant on the ability to use standard English. Morgan Job, a Minister of Parliament in Trinidad and Tobago, recently commented that schoolchildren in the islands must be instructed only in standard English (contrary to the recommendations made in the Education Policy Paper 1993–2003), since the use of the creole disadvantages them educationally, which has consequences for employment and social opportunities (*Trinidad Guardian* 19 June 1997).

Identical attitudes are evident elsewhere. Siegel (1993: 299–301) reports that creole-using ex-colonies in the Pacific, such as Melanesia, have also begun to move towards using indigenous languages in programmes of transitional bilingualism (again to standard English). Melanesia is one of the most linguistically diverse areas in the world, and it was recommended that the most widely known tongue, Melanesian Pidgin (of which there are three dialects: Tok Pisin in Papua New Guinea, Bislama in Vanautu and Pijin in the Solomon Islands) be used to teach initial literacy. However, this was met with reservations from a number of educationalists and administrators, who, echoing concerns voiced in Trinidad, 'feared that using a pidgin or creole based on English would interfere with the students' later acquisition of standard English' (1993: 299–301). Teachers too were reticent about the proposal. While they agreed that the use of Melanesian Pidgin would improve communication between themselves and the students, facilitate the latter's understanding of curriculum subjects, enable parents to participate more in their children's education and promote aspects of indigenous culture in the schools, 'over 90% of teachers surveyed were strongly in favour of English-only medium schools' (Nidue 1988: 226; quoted in Siegel 1993: 299–301).

The hurdle once again lay in challenging native speaker attitudes, the result of 'pro-English indoctrination'. It was difficult to 'convince many in the region that pidgins and creoles are not just 'broken English' or that they are suitable for formal education' (Siegel 1993: 299–301). Indeed, the current Minister of Education in Vanautu took Morgan Job's sentiments one step further and banned the use of Bislama (which has actually been declared the national language in the constitution) in high schools (even outside the classroom) and in the ministry offices (1993: 299–301).

Similarly, Hewitt (1989) states that when children of Afro-Caribbean ethnicity began attending schools in Britain (as a result of the large-scale immigrations from the Caribbean in the 1950s and 1960s), language policy did not initially accommodate to their needs, again because of English-centric attitudes:

> Their mother-tongue was conceived by educationalists and many parents alike as English or as a dialect of English and the relevant language issue here was thought to be one of 'interference' by Creole in their written and spoken production of the language (Wight 1969; Wight and Norris 1970). This ... was theoretically consistent with the traditionalist conservative political grammar associated with the view that Creole is bad or broken English; that the business of educational institutions is to promote high standards and that the presence of Creole or other dialects in the schools could only contribute to their decline.

> (Hewitt 1989: 127)[8]

One of the major obstacles to favourably changing attitudes towards the use of creoles in areas like education is 'the nature of linguistic diversity' (b2). English-lexifier creoles which draw a substantial proportion of their vocabulary and structure from the superstratal parent, and which possibly undergo decreolization processes (see Chapter 3) that generate mesolects close to the acrolectal variety (as well as the acrolect itself), therefore seem more English-like than creole-like. Creoles like TEC are, thus, in the minds of many, not sufficiently distinct from English to merit the status of an independent language. Like Melanesian Pidgin and London Jamaican, it is 'broken English', a 'Trinidad *dialect*' that is a mutilation of Oxford English (see page 110). Even the Education Policy Paper 1993–2003 refers to 'the dialect', complete with condemnatory quotation marks (see page 108)!

The 'developmental state' of languages like TEC (b3) also plays an important role in determining language attitudes. To make effective use of creoles in language planning strategies, even if only as a stepping stone to the acquisition of the official language, careful thought must be given to status and corpus planning. TEC, like many creoles, has no official status in the community. Its primary function as a 'home language'; its restricted use in local politics, in advertisements, cartoons and narratives with a local significance; its use as a transitional medium in schools all serve to sustain the belief that it is a 'grass roots' tongue, not fit for more 'serious' domains. The lack of corpus planning also reinforces this belief. TEC has no official grammars and dictionaries (apart from populist dictionaries such as *Cote Ce, Cote La* and *Trini Talk*). In addition, it has no systematic orthography: when it is represented in writing, it is often through an inconsistent modification of standard English orthography. For example, the TEC pronunciation of 'there' can be rendered in one text by both 'dere' and 'dey' as well as by its standard English spelling. Instability in spelling is therefore thought by some to indicate instability in the linguistic system itself; a conclusion that is further supported by the lack of grammars and dictionaries: if it has not been codified, it is obviously not worth writing in.

Corpus and status planning should therefore go hand in hand, since one seems to engender the other. However, 'in practice they belong to different professional domains; corpus planning being part of the professional domain of linguists and status planning being part of the professional domain of politics and/or authorities'. Both groups are in difficulties since 'linguists ... have no political power' and politicians 'generally have no (socio)linguistic knowledge' (Arends *et al.* 1995: 68), so the interchange of ideas necessary between the two groups is often non-existent.

The result is that recommendations such as those stated in Trinidad's Education Policy Paper cannot be carried out. The members of the National Task Force for Education appear to have no sociolinguistic knowledge, since they refer to TEC as a 'dialect', and also do not define the workings of the 'language policy' that will 'effectively utilize the "dialect"' in teaching literacy in standard English and 'address the development of an explicit awareness of the pupil's intuitive knowledge of "the dialect"'. Linguists such as Devonish (1986) and Winer (1990), on the other hand, have made proposals on codification issues. The former, for example, has advocated the use of a phonemic spelling system (that is, one that generally mirrors pronunciation) which could be based on the Cassidy Phonemic writing system, initially developed for Jamaica's English-lexifier creole and which 'has been used, with minor modifications for the representation of other English-lexicon creoles in the Caribbean by linguists' (Devonish 1986: 114). In terms of grammar and lexis, guides to the creole structures which are most frequently found across the continuum need to be researched and published. Processes of creole word-formation could also be used to present alternatives to English borrowings. These too would have to be authorized and published (Devonish 1986: 115–6). Winer (1990) makes recommendations only for an orthographic system for TEC. She considers the respective advantages and disadvantages of adopting either a phonemic spelling system, a historical–etymological system (which is heavily based on standard English orthography) or a modified English system (whereby standard English orthography would be used, but salient features of TEC pronunciation, such as [t] and [d] for <th>, would be consistently distinguished). Despite the fact that the use of a historical–etymological or modified English system impacts on the complicating issue of identity, in that both retain a 'subservience' to the colonial language, her final recommendation combines all three, with specific rules for usage:

1 Historically precedented and accepted forms can be used where known and available, and where they do not obscure pronunciation or etymology.
2 Phonemic orthography should be used for words: (a) for which there are no established historical precedents; (b) whose etyma are unknown; or (c) whose etyma are very different in form or phonology . . .
3 [discussed below]
4 Salient features within a text should be marked consistently, with variation indicating variation in language usage.
                                   (Adapted from Winer 1990: 263)

Her third recommendation, 'Apostrophes, quotation marks, or underlining should never be used to set off TEC words', links corpus and status planning by seeking to mitigate a perceived dependence on English: not signalling TEC as 'other' in writing may help to favourably change perceptions of it as a deviation from a norm.

So far, such suggestions have not been implemented. Thus, the bilingual materials and texts, grammars and dictionaries that are needed in schools if a transitional programme is to succeed, are non-existent. Consequently, Trinidad still wears the yoke of colonial language policy.

All stories of language planning policy in creole-speaking areas do not have the same ending, however. Siegel (1993: 302) cites the following examples.

HAITI

The island is home to a French-lexifier creole which has long been used in adult literacy programmes. In 1982, it was officially decreed the medium of instruction and made a subject of study for the first six years of primary education, again in a programme of transitional bilingualism. Requisite corpus planning was therefore carried out. However, evaluations carried out in 1983 and 1984 showed that competence in acquiring standard French had not improved (Benatolia 1987: 82; cited in Siegel 1993: 305). Attitudes towards the creole have remained negative, thus causing controversy over some aspects of codification, such as the adopted orthography (a phonemic spelling system), with which Dejeans (1993; quoted in Arends *et al.* 1995) states 90 per cent of teachers are unfamiliar.

SEYCHELLES, INDIAN OCEAN

The native creole here, Seselwa, also has a French-lexifier and has been used in education for many years. In the 1980s, it progressed from being a medium of instruction in initial literacy (again in a transitional bilingualism-to-French programme) to a subject of study in the first four years of primary education. Though the policy was practically identical to that implemented in Haiti, the outcome has been very different. Evaluations comparing the performance of grade 6 students in 1986 (the last class prior to the introduction of Seselwa as a medium of instruction) with those of 1987 (the first to be taught in Seselwa) showed that while grades were roughly even on English, in French the 1987 class achieved scores 12 per cent higher than the 1986 students. In Maths, they showed an increase of 4 per cent, Science 7 per cent and Social Studies 11 per cent. The seemingly universal fear that education through the medium of a creole would hinder academic progress has not, so far, been realized (Bickerton 1988: 3).

HAWAII

The native creole of this area is known as Hawaii Creole English. Though it received no official authorization to be used in schools, it was incoporated into the Kamehameha Early Education Program for part-Hawaiian children (Sato 1989; cited in Siegel 1993: 302). While standard English remained the primary medium of instruction, 'discourse strategies and participation structures used by Hawai'i Creole speakers were adopted by the program for use in the classroom' (Au 1980; cited in Siegel 1993). In 1987 the Hawaii Board of Education stated that only standard English should be spoken in the educational arena; but the strategies used in the Kamehameha Program seem to have achieved increased competence in the use of written and spoken standard English. It remains to be seen whether the educational authorities will modify their language policy in the light of this positive evaluation.

AUSTRALIA

The use of Northern Territory Creole, or Kriol, in education started in Barunga in 1975, through an experimental preschool programme. In 1977, the Northern Territory Department of Education began a formal transitional bilingual programme at the primary school. Kriol was used for reading and writing until grade 4 or 5, when English was introduced. The use of Kriol was thereafter restricted to subjects exploring local cultural heritage. In a 1982 evaluation of the success of this language policy, Murtaugh (1982; cited in Siegel 1993: 305) compared the oral language proficiency in Kriol and English of grades 1–3 students in the Barungan school with that of their native Kriol-speaking counterparts in an English-only school at Beswick Reserve. The scores of students at the bilingual school were significantly higher, especially in grade 3. Murtaugh (1982; cited in Siegel 1993: 305) states that the results 'indicate very definite trends towards the superiority of bilingual schooling over monolingual schooling for Creole-speaking students with regard to oral language proficiency in both the mother tongue, Creole, and the second language, English'.

All of the territories cited in this chapter share one major characteristic: they have all adopted transitional bilingualism programmes, in that the ultimate aim is to achieve competence in an international language. While the issue of language use in creole-speaking territories is intricately bound up with those of cultural independence and constructing a viable and autonomous New World identity, the historical shadows have not dissipated in the sunshine of political independence and, indeed, have lengthened under the force of practical considerations. As Arends *et al.* (1995: 66) point out, such 'societies betray a dualism in their language attitudes'; an inevitable inconsistency noted by McCrum *et al.* (1992: 347) in Jamaica, where the creole is indispensable as the voice of 'the Jamaican experience', but is seen as 'second-rate' in relation to (standard) English. Accordingly,

> Ask a Jamaican what he or she speaks and you will have the best expression of the paradox that underlies Caribbean attitudes towards English. ... Caribbean nationalism will prompt them to put as much distance as possible between what they speak and the Standard English of the ex-colonial visitor. On the other hand, if you suggest to the Jamaican that he or she does not speak English, they will be insulted or outraged.

> (McCrum *et al.* 1992: 348)

It would therefore seem that the use of creoles in official domains will continue to be restricted for some time to come, since 'inequality in the area of language [use] is but an expression of the social and economic inequality that exists' (Devonish 1986: 121). However, it is important to remember that these languages have survived as vibrant and adequate mediums of everyday communication for the majority of their speakers. Their story, then, unlike mine in this book, may not be over.

crick crack,

monkey break 'e back

for a piece of pommerac.

walk good.

Endnotes

1. Work on poetics and rhetoric never got off the ground; the grammar was started and abandoned, being taken up again only in the twentieth century. The dictionary was started immediately but the first edition was not published until 1694 (Cooper 1989: 11).
2. Many Caribbean territories achieved independence in the 1950s and 1960s.
3. *Zaboca* is derived from the last sound of *les* [z] being transferred to the beginning of *avocats*, the initial [lɛ] being elided, and word-medial [v] being replaced by [b].
4. The use of *bhaji* for 'spinach' is especially Trinidadian.

5. I am indebted to Professor Lise Winer (University of Illinois, Carbondale) for giving me copies of these texts when I couldn't find them in the national archives in Trinidad.

6. Social psychologists such as Lambert (1979) would term this *subtractive bilingualism,* a phenomenon whereby a speaker is forced to learn a high-status language and in so doing also absorbs all the values expressed in that language. As such, they learn to view their own language as inferior.

7. Craig (1980: 250–2) points out that the attainment of *monoliterate* and *partial bilingualism* is also often explicitly cited as the goal of language planning policies but that, ultimately, 'the goal of all three types of program [including the *transitional*] is literacy in the dominant, European language of education'.

8. Sebba (1997: 257–8) states that the British school system has come to recognize the fact that many pupils are creole users and so encourage writing in the creole and studying it as part of 'consciousness-raising' subjects; albeit to a limited extent. However, creole is no longer a sole mother tongue for many of these pupils (who, being British-born, tend to speak varieties of British English natively) and educational policy accordingly does not seek to make any language provision for these students, since it is assumed that they do not face a language barrier in the classroom.

Appendix

Trinidad Spectator, 8 November 1845 (see page 99)

Mr Editor – I calculate that the last palaver I sent you, was pretty considerably amusing to some of your folk; I take the liberty of sending you a little more of the same kind of gibberish, which you may use or abuse, as you think proper.

I am,

Jerry

Tacarigua, 27 October 1845

Scene: High Road; Kitty sitting, and Thomas advancing, limping and singing –

T: A la hack-a-bar-u
    Rack stone keep clear
    Jiggary foot da came.
    Massa Gobenar! who dis ya? da you Kit way maga so? you ben sick no?
K: Da te-day – little bit agen a ben da go kick-e-re-boo dis time.
T: Way you ben hab so no?
K: Me self no no – all me kin mask up, mash up eber since awee ben go na pa Billy danse de.
T: Dacta come see you?
K: Wish dacta? – way money da fu pay dacta? No madam John wa gib me all sort a bush fu bile.
T: Ah you drink tesan den?

K: Da little bit? – a drink tesan ta me self weary. Spose dacta bin come see me, he bin curse me, say da too much rum me drink.

T: Da true too, he no bin go tell bit lie neader – you da regular rum-sucker.

K: Ah! you begin, you begin – better lay me lone wee – da wid fu you money me da drink rum?

T: Eh-eh, eh-eh, d-o buddy, d-o – no begin cack up you calla bone gib me so, you no want yerry no-body talk bout you and da rum. Ayou topar blind lika bat; ebery day, ebery day, parsin da preachin gib ayou, an you cant yerry. You no see one man kill one tarra one na Cowra tarra day? – no rum? – all two a dem no ben drunk? Take care one day, one day, dem no mash you mout again like dem do terra day, cause da time you drink rum you like make yanga too much.

K: You no da drink rum no? you no memba da day da katchman buss you yey, because you hallar atter am when you bin drunk?

T: Wish katchman? – wa place? – wa time?

K: Ah! you want say you fougat now – you no memba da katch-man wid de lang nose – Missa-a way-you-call am – a fougat he name – you no memba?

T: Eh! Looko dey – da jackpaniar da come no he gig, keng-ger-ra – lay me go do; ef he come meet me ya wid dis cane, he go swear say da na fou he cane-piece a cut am – so lang. Me da go, go na Quamena wedding tomarra.

K: Ayou da go walk foot fou go na church?

T: Haff da go – go na gig, haff da ride pan mule, and tarra haff da go walk foot – me go ride me jack a has me.

Trinidad Guardian, 2 October 1827 (see page 99)

'*A Planter's Port Folio*' No. 2

Standing at my window one Sunday morning I overheard a conversation between two of my Negroes which was so interesting – larded with their quaint idioms and humorous proverbs, expressed in those most ludicrous dialects, negro English and creole French, that I with difficulty refrained from laughter. The substance of this earnest colloquy I found to be a little domestic *faux-pas* – occurrences which take place every day among your favourite Blackies, in spite of your high opinion of their *moral* capabilities. Quaco related to Cudjoe his having been a great distance, and on his return, found in the house of Mimba (his favourite sultana, for whom he had repudiated three other wives) long John, a Kind of half-tailor belonging to a neighbouring plantation. A scuffle took place, in which, the tailor, according to Quashie's account, came off second-best. Poor Quashie told the tale of his jealousy, his affray with long John, and his reproof of Mimba, in such a curious way, embroidering his account with such laughable adages and extraordinary similes, that after the dialogue ceased, I was seized with one of those rhyming fits, which, in common with all men – Poets or not – I am subject to, and resolved to try how Quashie's story would look in verse, using his own dialect. These verses I send you, begging your indulgence (as you are not a Trinidad Planter) for any obscurity which may appear in them, and the want of good rhymes, which are not easily found in so mixed and imperfect a patois as the following are composed in.

Yours, &c.

Matthew Muscovado

*It may be necessary to inform the reader, that the greater part of the papers under the title of 'A Planter's Port Folio' are extracts from copies of letters written, and a journal kept during a long residence in Trinidad and a voyage home. Ed.

Quaco and Mimba
(A Negro Ballad)

'Where about you bin go to a'day?
Me no see you n'yie massa nigger!'
'Me bin walk so, one hell-ob-a-way,
All a'way till we meet up Dry Ribber.'

'And wha' for you look for so black?
You heart burn, no so bex, Buddy Quaco?'
'Compe'e Cudjoe, me meet, coming back,
Someting chook for my kin like one fork O!

'Anty Mimba me no tink tan such,
Wha she do make me bex till me blue oui,
Wen you say she go lobe man too much,
You bin put goat mout pon her for true oui!

'Yam-yam no bin dare, fire bin out,
Me look so behind her bamboo dae;
What you tink say me see peepin out?
One great big foot finger for true dare.

'Me Mimba no sabby make fool,
Me swear dat me no know wha hale her;
Who you tink me find under de stool?
Dat ugly-face long John de tailor!

'He face tan like Jumbee-bird Owl,
(For true, he bin dam ug'y feller),
He mout tan like Hog da yam fowl,
He Crapeau yie shine like two dollar.

'Him imp'rence feller of course,
Da Gobbener self no talk bigger;
Buckra servant (you know) ride big Horse!
He saucy for true like one Chigger.

'Me look him – he gie much such law –
Gorramighty! him no tink me butt him.
When me hold him, me top for him jaw –
Catch him hold him two ear so, an butt him.

'Like cockroach run way from one Fowl,
When me butt him wid fist he da run O!
Me box him wid foot till he howl
Like Sloth in a wood – *Poor me one O!*

'At last him take road, run way –
Da Gootee self neber run fasser:
I bin follow him spose he bin day,
But night no hab yie, no hab Massa.'

'Wha for you no curse Mimba no?
You no quarrel her no, Buddy Quaco?'
'Me say – Wha for Mimba do so?
Dis de way you na make when me walk O!

'No me tief for you till me get flog?
For you me broke stone, sell me tannia.
No for you me sell fowl, goat and hog;
My plantain, pease, cush-cush, bannana?

'No for you me bin buy Madras grand?
(Da yangar you wear, wha dem cost you?)
Wite tockin for foot and for hand,
Ear-ring hebby and big like one hoss-shoe!

'Tree wife me been hab; no for you
Me take myself from dem and gie you?
And now when me go walk (for true)
Da dam long John de Tailor come see you.'

'Softly softly catch Monkey wa' so
Buddy Quaco,' she say, 'keep dis bodder,
All dis time you no sabby me no!
Don't you know Tailor John da my brodder?'
'Spose you tink to fool Quaco dat way,
Mimba better go look out for odder;
If me find Musheer wid you, you say
(Gorramighty 'na top) him you modder.'

Glossary

analytic: a language type in which grammatical relationships are shown primarily (if not completely) through word order, not inflections. An example of such a sentence in English (now a highly analytic language) is *the child may stroke the cat*, where the order of the constituents signals which determiner goes with which noun; that auxiliary *may* modifies the main verb *stroke*; that *the child* is the subject of the verb and *the cat*, the direct object.

assimilation: a phonological process whereby sounds are made more similar in their articulation. Take for example, the pronunciation of a word such as *handbag*. Many English speakers typically will not enunciate the 'middle *d*', thus producing [hanbag] *<hanbag>*. However, in rapid and/or informal speech, this will sometimes become *<hambag>*. In *<hanbag>*, a nasal sound where the tip of the tongue is placed on the alveolar ridge (*n* [n]: alveolar nasal) precedes one where the lips are brought together before air is pushed out of the mouth (*b* [b]: bilabial plosive). In *<hambag>*, the speaker assimilates the sounds so that they are closer in articulation: [n] is replaced by [m], a bilabial nasal, which is 'nearer' to the following bilabial plosive [b].

calque: typically a word or phrase which has been borrowed from one language by another; but which has been translated literally into the borrowing language. Thus, the English *superman* is a direct translation of the German *Übermensch*. Similarly, TEC *it makin' cold* is a calque of French/French-lexifier creole *il fait froid* literally 'it makes cold'.

case: a grammatical category which signals, often through inflections, the syntactic relationship between words in a sentence. In Old

English (449–1100), for example, many nouns would carry inflections that indicated whether they were in *nominative case* (typically functioning as a subject; as in *se oxa* 'the ox' nominative singular); *accusative case* (typically functioning as direct object; as in *thone oxan* 'the ox' accusative singular); *genitive case* (possessive; as in *thaes oxan* 'the ox's' genitive singular) and *dative case* (indirect object; as in *thaem oxan* '(to) the ox' dative singular) (Pyles and Algeo 1982: 113–15). As can be seen, not only do the nouns carry case marking but so do the determiners, which are inflected to agree with the case of the noun (as well as with its number and gender; see **grammatical gender**, below).

codification: the process whereby rules for usage (typically for a standard variety) are set out in reference works such as dictionaries, grammar books, spelling and pronunciation guides.

cognate: a term used in historical linguistics to describe lexical items in different languages which are similar in structure and meaning, not because of borrowing but because of genetic relatedness. Thus, English and French both have words such as *prince, castle* and *army* but they are not cognate, since the former language borrowed such cultural terms from the French after the Norman Conquest. However, languages such as English, Latin, Welsh and Greek share similarities in their basic vocabulary, as can be seen in number terms such as *one, two* and *three* (Latin *unus, duo, tres;* Welsh *un, dau, tri;* Greek *oine, duo, treis*). Since it is unlikely that these languages borrowed such everyday terms from each other, it is highly possible that such correspondences are due instead to these *cognate* forms having been derived from a common ancestor. Languages that share a common ancestor are also referred to as *cognate*: the term does not apply only to *lexical items* in those languages.

comparative reconstruction: a method used in historical linguistics to *reconstruct* past stages in linguistic evolution, by *comparing* data such as cognates (see above) in order to work backwards to an ancestral form. Thus, by comparing cognates in languages such as Germanic, Celtic and Italic, for example, and by working out the rules of change that may have applied, linguists have been able to reconstruct forms that may have been used in their mother, Proto-Indo-European. Historical linguists also make use of **internal reconstruction** (see below).

CVCV: a notation used to denote sequences with a consonant (C) vowel (V) structure.

diachronic: a term used in linguistics to describe language change *through* time. For example, an examination of how English changed between AD 600 and AD 1350 would be a diachronic study.

grammatical gender: this can be seen in languages where nouns, for example, carry gender and all noun modifiers must carry grammatical agreement. For example, the nouns in modern-day languages such as French and Spanish carry masculine or feminine gender. Modifying determiners and adjectives *must* carry agreement with this gender (particularly in the singular form), as in French *le chat noir* 'the black cat' (masculine) but *la table noire* 'the black table' (feminine); Spanish *el gato blanco* 'the white cat' (masculine) and *la mesa blanca* 'the white table' (feminine).

generative linguistics: an approach to linguistic analysis spearheaded by Noam Chomsky, in reaction to **structural linguistics** (see below). The main idea underlying a *generative* approach is that the brain's **Language Acquisition Device** (see below) lodges a finite set of rules which *generate* the infinite number of utterances of which the native speaker of a language is capable.

grammaticalization: a process whereby words with 'full semantic content' lose their independent meaning and come instead to serve as a marker of a grammatical function. For example, the verb *save/savvy* in Tok Pisin has a 'full' meaning of 'to know how to', but is being *grammaticalized* to *sa*, which is prefixed on to verbs and denote habitual aspect (Holm 1988 : 161).

Hamitic: the name of the language family that comprises the *Nilo-Saharan*, *Niger-Khorfodian* and *Khoisan* languages of Africa (see Pyles and Algeo 1982: 67 for more detail).

internal reconstruction: a methodology typically used in historical linguistics to reconstruct past stages in a language's evolution, by only using data from *that* language (as opposed to **comparative reconstruction**, see above). For example, we could reconstruct the processes by which a particular sound change took place in English between 1400–1600 by looking only at relevant English data.

koineization: a process which typically takes place in a community initially consisting of speakers of related dialects, who then 'get rid of' many non-shared features and 'keep' those that are similar across the lects. For example, Trinidad received 145 000 immigrants from India in the late nineteenth century, the majority of whom spoke dialects of Bhojpuri. The Indian community appears to have 'levelled' out many of the distinctive features of these dialects, and the result has been a Bhojpuri koine, which is still in use today (Holm 1989: 460).

labialized: an articulation of a sound which includes lip (*labia*) rounding. For example, in the articulation of *shoe,* the initial <*sh*> [ʃ] is often pronounced with a certain measure of lip rounding because of the following rounded vowel [u].

Language Acquisition Device: a term coined by Noam Chomsky to denote what seems to be the innate human faculty for acquiring language.

language death: a phenomenon whereby a language falls out of use or changes radically under the influence of another. Language death can occur because of the physical death of a speech community; or because speakers abandon their native language for an unrelated but prestigious tongue in the community (*language murder*); or because speakers take on features of a related and superimposed language, thus changing the structure of their native tongue (*language suicide*). These terms are more fully explained in Chapter 4.

lexifier: a term for the language in a creole-formation environment which supplies the majority of the creole's lexicon. The lexifier is typically the **superstratal** language (see below).

linguistic prescriptivism: a term used to denote the formulation of rules for language use, in both the written and spoken medium. Modern linguistics aims to be *descriptive* in its approach (that is, to *describe* what users of a language do). However, rules of usage are often devised for use of standard varieties, for example. Standard English is one such, with many rules for use in the written medium (such as no split infinitives, no double negation, no 'dangling' prepositions at the end of sentences) having first been *prescribed* by eighteenth-century grammarians anxious to 'refine' the language (see Chapter 4).

morphosyntax: a term used to denote the interplay between the *morphological* (word formation) and *syntactic* (structural) components of a language's grammatical system. For example, plural marking in nouns in English can be described as a *morphosyntactic* category: the plural inflection '-s' is a morphological feature which affects syntax, in that a pluralized noun subject, for example, will require a plural form of the verb, as well as anaphoric plural pronouns (if applicable); as in *the boys are eating their dinner* (adapted from Crystal 1980: 226).

nominalizer: a morpheme which creates a noun from a member of another word class. For example, the *nominalizer* <-er> creates the noun *teacher* from the verb *teach*.

phonotactic: a term used to describe the phonological sequences that occur in a language. For example, we could say that a (made up) word such as *ngefh* does not conform to the *phonotactic* rules of English, a language in which the sequence <ng> [ŋ] does not occur word-initially and <fh> does not occur at all.

structuralist linguistics: a term used to denote linguistic analysis that concentrates on describing features in terms of *structures* or *systems* (also known as *structural linguistics*). In *structuralist linguistics*, the emphasis lies on deconstructing, or breaking down, and classifying the 'physical' features of utterances. It is an approach that was criticized by Chomsky, who introduced the concepts of **generative linguistics** (see above).

substratal: a term used to denote the strata of a community that carries little or no socio-political power (*sub* 'under' + *strata* 'level'). The language(s) of this group in a creole-formation environment is known as the substrate (indicating, if there are many languages, that they are essentially similar systems) or substrata (indicating that the languages are, in essence, very distinct from each other).

superstratal: a term used to denote the strata of a community that carries socio-political power (*super* 'above' + *strata* 'level'). Their language in a creole-formation environment is known as the superstrate (indicating that just one dialect/variety of a language is present, or that the variation among the dialects/varieties present is not distinctive) or superstratum (indicating that more than one dialect/

variety of the language is in use, and that the variation between them is distinctive). The superstratal language in a creole-formation environment is also known as the **lexifier** (see above).

synchronic: a term used in linguistics to describe the study of language variation at a particular point in time. For example, a study on differences in pronoun usage in varieties of contemporary English is synchronic.

synthetic: a language type in which grammatical relationships are primarily expressed by changing the internal structure of words, typically by the use of inflectional endings. An example of *synthesis* in an English sentence can be seen in *the prettiest girl's handwriting was also the neatest. Prettiest* and *neatest* carry the superlative adjectival inflection <*-est*> (and describe the girl who has the most of both these qualities); *girl* carries the possessive <*-'s*> inflection (indicating her 'possession' of her handwriting); and the verb *was* is derived from *to be*, inflected for past tense.

TEC: Trinidad's English-lexifer Creole.

Bibliography

Aitchison, J. (1981). *Language Change: Progress or Decay?* Fontana: London.

—— (1983). On roots of language. *Language and Communication* 3, pp. 83–97.

Alleyne, M. (1971). Acculturation and the Cultural Matrix of Creolization. In D. Hymes (ed.) *Pidginization and Creolization of Languages*. Cambridge: Cambridge University Press, pp. 169–86.

—— (1980). *Comparative Afro-American*. Ann Arbor: Karoma.

Arends, J., P. Muysken and N. Smith (eds) (1995). *Pidgins and Creoles: An Introduction*. Amsterdam: John Benjamins.

Bailey, B.L. (1966). *Jamaican Creole Syntax: a Transformational Approach*. Cambridge: Cambridge University Press.

Baker, P. and C. Corne. (1982). *Isle de France Creole: Affinities and Origins*. Ann Arbor: Karoma.

Bakker, P. and M. Mous. (1994). *Materials on Mixed Languages*. Amsterdam: IFOTT.

Baugh, A.C. and T. Cable (1978). *A History of the English Language*. New Jersey: Prentice Hall, Inc.

Bickerton, D. (1973). On the Nature of a Creole Continuum. *Language* 49, pp. 641–9.

—— (1974). Creolization, Linguistic Universals, Natural Semantax and the Brain. In R. Day (ed.) *Issues in English Creoles*. Heidelberg: Julius Groos, pp. 1–18.

—— (1975). *Dynamics of a Creole System*. Cambridge: Cambridge University Press.

—— (1977). Pidginization and Creolization: language acquisition and language universals. In A. Valdman (ed.) *Pidgin and Creole Linguistics*. Bloomington: Indiana University Press, pp. 49–69.

—— (1981). *Roots of Language*. Ann Arbor: Karoma Publishers Ltd.

—— (1986). The Sociohistorical Matrix of Creolization. *Journal of Pidgin and Creole Languages* 7:2, pp. 307–18.

—— (1988). Creole Languages and the Bioprogram. In F.J. Newmeyer (ed.) *Linguistics: The Cambridge Survey*, vol. I. Cambridge: Cambridge University Press, pp. 268–84.

—— and P. Muysken. (1988). A Dialog Concerning the Linguistic Status of Creole Languages. In F.J. Newmeyer (ed.) *Linguistics: The Cambridge Survey*, vol. I. Cambridge: Cambridge University Press, pp. 302–6.

Brathwaite, E. (1967). *The Arrivants: A New World Trilogy*. Oxford: Oxford University Press.

Byrne, F. and J. Holm (eds) (1993). *Atlantic meets Pacific – a Global View of Pidginization and Creolization*. Amsterdam: John Benjamins Publishing Company.

Carrington, L.D. (1992). Images of Creole Space. *Journal of Pidgin and Creole Languages* 7:1, pp. 93–9.

Chaudenson, R. (1974). *Le Lexique du parler créole de la Réunion*. Paris: Champion.

Christian, D. (1988). Language Planning: The View from Linguistics. In F.J. Newmeyer (ed.) *Linguistics: The Cambridge Survey*, vol. I. Cambridge: Cambridge University Press, pp. 193–209.

Cobarrubias, J. and J.A. Fishman (eds) (1983). *Progress in Language Planning: International Perspectives*. Berlin: Mouton.

Cooper, R. (1989). *Language Planning and Social Change*. Cambridge: Cambridge University Press.

Coulmas, F. (ed.) (1997). *The Handbook of Sociolinguistics*. Oxford: Basil Blackwell.

Craig, D. (1971). Education and Creole English in the West Indies: Some Sociolinguistic Factors. In D. Hymes (ed.) *Pidginization and Creolization of Languages*. Cambridge: Cambridge University Press, pp. 371–92.

—— (1980). Models for Education Policy in Creole-Speaking Communities. In A. Valdman and A. Highfield (eds) *Theoretical Orientations in Creole Studies*. New York: Academic Press, pp. 245–66.

Crowley, T. (1991). *Beach la Mar to Bislama*. Oxford: Oxford University Press.

Crystal, D. (1980). *A Dictionary of Linguistics and Phonetics*. Oxford: Blackwell.

Daoust, D. (1997). Language Planning and Language Reform. In F. Coulmas (ed.) *The Handbook of Sociolinguistics*. Oxford: Basil Blackwell, pp. 437–55.

Day, R. (1980). *Issues in English Creoles.* Heidelberg: Julius Groos.

de Boissière, R. (1952). *Crown Jewel.* London: Picador.

DeCamp, D. (1971). Towards a Generative Analysis of a Post Creole Speech Continnum. In D. Hymes (ed.) *Pidginization and Creolization of Languages.* Cambridge: Cambridge University Press, pp. 349–70.

Devonish, H. (1986). *Language and Liberation: Creole Language Politics in the Caribbean.* London: Karia Press.

Dillard, J.L. (1970). Principles in the History of American English: Paradox, Virginity, and Cafeteria. *Florida Foreign Language Reporter* 8, pp. 32–3.

Douglas, M. (1996 (1966)). *Purity and Danger: An Analysis of the Concepts of Pollution and Taboo.* London: Routledge.

Duechar, M. (1987). Sign Languages as Creoles and Chomsky's Notion of Universal Grammar. In S. Modgil and C. Modgil (eds) *Noam Chomsky: Consensus and Controversy.* Brighton: Falmer Press.

Farrar, K.J. (1996). *The Role of Contact in the Explanation of Syntactic Change.* PhD dissertation. Cambridge University.

Fasold, R.W. (1984). *The Sociolinguistics of Language.* Oxford: Basil Blackwell.

Fishman, J.A., C.A. Ferguson and J. Das Gupta (eds) (1968). *Language Problems of Developing Nations.* New York/London/Sydney/Toronto: John Wiley and Sons, Inc.

Foley, W.A. (1988). Language Birth: The Processes of Pidginization and Creolization. In F.J. Newmeyer (ed.) *Linguistics: The Cambridge Survey.* Cambridge: Cambridge University Press, pp. 162–83.

Gal, S. (1979) *Language Shift.* New York: Academic Press.

Giles, H. and R. St Clair (eds) (1979). *Language and Social Psychology.* Oxford: Basil Blackwell.

Görlach, M. (1985). Lexicographical Problems of New Englishes and English Related Pidgin and Creole Languages. *English World-Wide* 6:1, pp. 1–33.

Grillo, R. (ed.) (1989). *Social Anthropology and the Politics of Language.* London: Routledge.

Hall, R.A. (1966). *Pidgin and Creole Languages.* Ithaca: Cornell University Press.

Hancock, I.F. (1986). The Domestic Hypothesis, Diffusion and Componentiality: An Account of Atlantic Anglophone Creole Origins. In P. Muysken and N. Smith (eds) *Substrata vs. Universals in Creole Genesis.* Amsterdam: John Benjamins, pp. 71–102.

Haynes, M. (1987). *Trinidad and Tobago Dialect (Plus)*. San Fernando, Trinidad: Martin Haynes.

Hewitt, R. (1989). Creole in the Classroom: Political Grammars and Educational Vocabularies. In R. Grillo (ed.) *Social Anthropology and the Politics of Language*. London: Routledge, pp. 127–44.

Holm, J. (1988). *Pidgins and Creoles*, vol. I: *Theory and Structure*. Cambridge: Cambridge University Press.

—— (1989). *Pidgins and Creoles*, vol. II: *Reference Survey*. Cambridge: Cambridge University Press.

Horizon (1997). *Silent Children; New Language*. London: BBC.

Hymes, D. (1971). *Pidginization and Creolization of Languages*. Cambridge: Cambridge University Press.

Ihalainen, O. (1991). Periphrastic *Do* in Affirmative Sentences in the Dialect of East Somerset. In P. Trudgill and J.K. Chambers (eds) *Dialects of English: Studies in Grammatical Variation*. Essex: Longman Group UK Limited, pp. 148–60.

Jespersen, O. (1922). *Language: Its Nature, Development and Origin*. London: Allen and Unwin.

Joseph, T. (1999). Wendy Lets Her Hair Down ... and Crowd Fails to Recognise Her. *Trinidad Express*, 9 May.

Keens-Douglas, P. (1984). *Lal Shop*. Port of Spain: Keensdee Productions.

Labov, W. (1972). *Language in the Inner City*. Philadelphia: University of Pennsylvania Press.

Lambert, W.E. (1979). Language as a factor in intergroup relations. In H. Giles and R. St Clair (eds) *Language and Social Psychology*. Oxford: Basil Blackwell, pp. 186–92.

Le Page, R.B. (1968). Problems to be Faced in the Use of English as the Medium of Instruction in Four West Indian Territories. In J.A. Fishman, C.A. Ferguson and J. Das Gupta (eds) *Language Problems of Developing Nations*. New York/London/Sydney/Toronto: John Wiley and Sons, Inc., pp. 431–42.

—— (1978). 'Projection, focussing, diffusion' or, steps toward a sociolinguistic theory of language, illustrated from the sociolinguistic survey of multilingual communities, States I: Cayo District, Belize (formerly British Honduras) and II: St Lucia. School of Education, St Augustine, Trinidad: Society for Caribbean Linguistics Occasional Paper No. 9.

—— and A. Tabouret-Keller (1985). *Acts of Identity: Creole based approaches to language and ethnicity*. Cambridge: Cambridge University Press.

Lovelace, E. (1965). *While Gods are Falling*. London: Longman.

McCrum, R., W. Cran and R. MacNeil (1992). *The Story of English*. London: Faber and Faber Limited and BBC Books.

McMahon, A. (1994). *Understanding Language Change*. Cambridge: Cambridge University Press.

Mendes, J. (1986). *Cote Ce, Cote La: Trinidad and Tobago Dictionary*. Arima, Trinidad: John Mendes.

Meillet, A. (1967). *The Comparative Method in Historical Linguistics*. Paris: Champion.

Modgil, S. and C. Modgil (eds) (1987). *Noam Chomsky: Consensus and Controversy*. Brighton: Falmer Press.

Mühlhäusler, P. (1986). *Pidgin and Creole Linguistics*. Oxford: Basil Blackwell.

Muysken, P. (1988). Are Creoles a Special Type of Language? In F.J. Newmeyer (ed.) *Linguistics: The Cambridge Survey*, vol. I. Cambridge: Cambridge University Press, pp. 285–301.

Muysken, P. and D. Bickerton (1988). The linguistic status of creole languages: two perspectives. In F.J. Newmeyer (ed.) *Linguistics: The Cambridge Survey*, vol. II. Cambridge. Cambridge University Press, pp. 267–306.

Muysken, P. and N. Smith. (1986). *Substrata vs. Universals in Creole Genesis*. Amsterdam: John Benjamins.

Naro, A.J. (1978). A Study on the Origins of Pidginization. *Language* 54:2, pp. 314–49.

National Task Force on Education. *Education Policy Paper (1993–2003): White Paper*. Trinidad: Ministry of Education.

Newmeyer, F.J. (1988). *Linguistics: The Cambridge Survey*, vols I and II. Cambridge: Cambridge University Press.

Niles, N.A. (1980). *Provincial English Dialects and Barbadian English*. PhD dissertation, University of Michigan: Ann Arbor.

O'Donnell, W.R. and L. Todd (1980). *Variety in Contemporary English*. London: Allen and Unwin.

Pyles, T. and J. Algeo (1982). *The Origins and Development of the English Language*. New York: Harcourt Brace Jovanovich.

Rae, J. (1982). The decline and fall of English grammar. *Observer*, 7 February.

Reinecke, J.E. (1937). *Marginal Languages: a Sociological Survey of the Creole Languages and Trade Jargons*. PhD dissertation, Yale University. Ann Arbor: University Microfilms International.

Rice, F.A. (ed.) (1962). *Study of the Role of Second Languages in Asia, Africa and Latin America*. Washington: Center for Applied Linguistics.

Rickford, J.R. (1986). Social Contact and Linguistic Diffusion: Hiberno-English and New World Black English. *Language* 62:2, pp. 245–89.

—— (1987). *Dimensions of a Creole Continnum: History, Texts and Linguistic Analysis of Guyanese Creole.* Stanford: Stanford University Press.

Romaine, S. (1988). *Pidgin and Creole Languages.* London: Longman.

Rushdie, S. (1990). *Haroun and the Sea of Stories.* London: Granta Books.

Sebba, M. (1997). *Contact Languages: Pidgins and Creoles.* Hampshire and London: MacMillan Press Ltd.

Siegel, J. (1993). Pidgins and Creoles in Education in Australia and the Southwest Pacific. In F. Byrne and J. Holm (eds) *Atlantic meets Pacific – a Global View of Pidginization and Creolization.* Amsterdam: John Benjamins Publishing Company.

Singh, I. (1991). *The Influence of Early Modern English on the Trinidadian English-based Creole.* MPhil. dissertation: Cambridge University.

—— (1997). *Superstratal Influence on the Formation of Trinidad's English-based Creole.* Unpublished PhD dissertation: Cambridge University.

Smith, K. (1999). Pride of a Lion. *Trinidad Express,* 13 July.

Stewart, W.A. (1962). Creole Languages in the Caribbean. In F.A. Rice (ed.) *Study of the Role of Second Languages in Asia, Africa and Latin America.* Washington: Center for Applied Linguistics, pp. 34–53.

Taylor, D.R. (1956). Language Contacts in the West Indies. *Word* 7, pp. 43–59.

—— (1959). On function words versus form in 'non-traditional' languages. *Word* 15, pp. 485–589.

Thomason, S. and T. Kaufman (1988). *Language Contact, Creolization and Genetic Linguistics.* Berkeley: University of California Press.

Todd, L. (1974). *Pidgins and Creoles.* London, Boston: Routledge and Kegan Paul.

Tollefson, J.W. (1991). *Planning Language, Planning Inequality: Language Policy in the Community.* Harlow: Longman.

Trudgill, P. (1983). *On Dialect.* Oxford: Basil Blackwell.

—— and J.K. Chambers (eds) (1991). *Dialects of English: Studies in Grammatical Variation.* Essex: Longman Group UK Limited.

Valdman, A. (ed.) (1977) *Pidgin and Creole Linguistics*. Bloomington: Indiana University Press.

Valdman, A. and A. Highfield (1980). *Theoretical Orientations in Creole Studies*. New York: Academic Press.

Wallace, L. (1979). Language as a Factor in Inter-Group Relations. In H. Giles and R. St Clair (eds) *Language and Social Psychology*. Oxford: Basil Blackwell.

Washabaugh, W. (1977). Constraining Variation in Decreolization. *Language* 53:2, pp. 329–52.

Watts, D. (1987). *The West Indies: Patterns of Development, Culture and Environmental Change since 1492*. Cambridge: Cambridge University Press.

Werner. J. (1995). *The Beak of the Finch*. UK: Jonathan Cape Ltd.

Whinnom, K. (1956). *Spanish Contact Vernaculars in the Philippine Islands*. Hong Kong: Hong Kong University Press.

—— (1971). Linguistic Hybridization and the 'Special Case' of Pidgins and Creoles. In D. Hymes (ed.) *Pidginization and Creolization of Languages*. Cambridge: Cambridge University Press, pp. 91–115.

Winer, L. (1990). Orthographic Standardization for Trinidad and Tobago: Linguistic Sociopolitical Considerations in an English Creole Community. *Language Problems and Language Planning* 14:3, pp. 237–68.

—— (1993). *Varieties of English Around the World: Trinidad and Tobago*. Amsterdam/Philadelphia: John Benjamins Publishing Company.

Winford, D. (1997). Creole Studies and Sociolinguistics. *Journal of Pidgin and Creole Languages* 12:2, pp. 302–18.

ADDITIONAL NEWSPAPER ARTICLES

'Courses for Teachers: From Our Files (60 years ago)' *Trinidad Guardian* 14 July 1997.

'Evidence in Patois: From Our Files (75 years ago)' *Trinidad Guardian* 7 July 1997.

'Job Stands by English Statement' *Trinidad Guardian* 19 June 1997.

Index